The Practical Guide to Facilitation

A Self-Study Resource

John Farrell   **Richard Weaver**

BERRETT-KOEHLER PUBLISHERS, INC.
San Francisco

Human Resource Development Press

Published by:

HRD Press
22 Amherst Road
Amherst, MA 01002
1-800-822-2801 (U.S. and Canada)
413-253-3488
413-253-3490 (FAX)
www.hrdpress.com

Berrett-Koehler
450 Sansome Street, Suite 1200
San Francisco, CA 94111

415-288-0260
415-362-2512 (FAX)
www.bkconnection.com

Printed in Canada

ISBN 1-57675-095-7

Cover design by Eileen Klockars
Editorial services by Robie Grant
Production services by Clark T. Riley

Dedication

To Laurie, my wife, my love, my friend.
John

To Patti, my constant source of support and love.
Richard

Table of Contents

Preface

After we wrote *Managers as Facilitators* (Berrett-Koehler Publishers), people continued to tell us about the success they were achieving using the role of facilitator. They were finding that using our definition of facilitation — helping people get their work done and improve the way they work together — was yielding necessary and welcome results.

The professional managers that we trained to use the role of facilitator were getting their projects done faster while helping their teams improve performance. Even though this facilitation training was producing dramatic improvements, fitting time for training into an increasingly tight schedule was becoming nearly impossible. Managers asked us to deliver a self-study workbook that would make it possible to learn the role of facilitator through independent study. This is that workbook.

Inside *The Practical Guide to Facilitation* you will find a study program that creates the learning experience similar to the one we provide as consultants and trainers.

The Practical Guide to Facilitation can be used as a stand-alone workbook, but you will find our book, *Managers as Facilitators*, to be a helpful additional reference.

We have been very deliberate in our choice of a fitness metaphor for this workbook. We see facilitation as a role that requires constant use. You have to keep your facilitation muscles toned and in shape. This workbook will help you do that.

How to Use This Workbook

This workbook contains an Introduction and nine units that should be completed sequentially. The Introduction contains a facilitation skills self-assessment that will help you understand your strengths and weaknesses. You can use the results to help you focus your work through the self-study program. After completing each unit you will have finished specific tasks that will help you successfully use the role of facilitator. You can complete each unit at your own pace.

At the beginning of each unit is a "**Warm-up**." The warm-up describes in detail the things you have to learn to complete that unit. The warm-up also alerts you to the things you have to observe, think about, and do in order to be proficient with that unit's particular aspect of facilitation. It provides descriptions of models and concepts that you will apply in each unit. In other words, the warm-up indicates the "muscle groups" you will work out.

Each unit also contains a number of "**Facilitation Work-outs**" that will ask you to exercise your head, heart, and hands in order to improve your skills. Each Facilitation Work-out contains two parts:

- **Preparation**: A short text summary that provides information you need to complete the exercises that follow.
- **Exercises**: Worksheets that require you to record your observations, answer questions, take notes about your conversations with others, and facilitate work with groups.

The exercises are classified with up to three different icons that explain the nature of each. Some exercises ask for an immediate response. Others need more indepth study and reflection, often requiring you to observe people and situations in your workplace. Other exercises expect you to facilitate work with a group. The icons representing each classification of exercise are shown below.

Icon 1.
Respond to questions right away.

Icon 2.
Study your workplace, talk with others, and record your observations.

Icon 3.
Facilitate work with a group.

At the end of each unit is a "**Cool-down**" that will help you integrate that unit's particular aspects of facilitation into the overall facilitation model. The purpose of the Cool-down is to help you:

1. Assess your mastery of the subject matter of each unit
2. Make an action plan for using what you have learned to improve your productivity

The title of each Facilitation Work-out reappears in this Cool-down section. We have found that taking this additional step with the material will get your facilitation muscles in top condition.

Acknowledgments

This book is all about collaboration — people working together. In our work together as authors and consultants, we have found the collaborative approach to be immensely productive and rewarding. When we encountered the inevitable challenges everyone meets in working with others, we used the very material in this book to help us stay on task *and* strengthen our relationship.

One particularly important challenge we faced was deciding upon whose name would appear first on this book. This is a nontrivial consideration because of the assumptions that others make about the "first" and "second" author of any book. We want our readers to know that our work is truly co-owned by both of us. We do not focus on individual contribution. What is important to us is that we continue to improve our material so that it is more useful and helpful to others. This is what our collaboration is all about.

Thus, you will see John Farrell as the first author of *The Practical Guide to Facilitation* and Richard Weaver as the first author of *Managers as Facilitators*. We decided to alternate the order of author because that feels fair to us. Fairness is one of the most important values we hold in our working partnership. Our commitment to each other, and our belief in the power of collaboration, helped us make this decision.

Of course, we again called upon our friends and colleagues to help us improve this book. We especially want to recognize Patti Christensen who contributed significantly to this work. Patti read the manuscript several times and provided valuable advice and insight that helped make it better. Our test readers, David Anderson, Peggy Christensen, Madeline Finnerty, Sharon Hillestad, Margaret Jennings, and Ryan Kanne, helped us improve the manuscript in a number of important ways. Our colleagues, Ann Jones, Patti Christensen (instrument testers), helped us test and refine our facilitation skills instrument. In addition, Steve Piersanti and the rest of the staff at Berrett-Koehler Publishers, Inc., did their usual outstanding job in helping us put together another book that we feel will help people be more successful in their work and in their lives. Our new publisher, HRD Press, provided outstanding support to this work. We especially want to acknowledge Chris Hunter, Robie Grant, and Eileen Klockars.

The success of *Managers as Facilitators* has been tremendously rewarding. We wish to thank all of you who have used it to improve your workplaces. To have so many people from such diverse organizations report back their satisfaction and success with our material has been truly gratifying. To have them ask for more is an even greater honor.

This workbook helps us continue our quest to help people use the role of facilitator to improve their workplaces, strengthen their relationships, and achieve their goals. We emerge from this latest project with a stronger professional and personal relationship and a renewed commitment to our mutual success. Equally important, we remain committed to helping you make your workplace better.

Introduction:
Assessing Your Facilitation Skills

Welcome to *The Practical Guide to Facilitation*. This rigorous exercise program will help you develop your facilitation skills. If you have recently started exploring how to use the role of facilitator, this guide will help you build a firm foundation of skills and knowledge. If you are an experienced facilitator, you will be given the opportunity to deepen your understanding and broaden your application of the art and science of facilitation.

The Facilitation Skills Self-Assessment instrument that follows will help you understand your current skill level. You will earn several ratings that will indicate both your overall "facilitation fitness level" and the strength and flexibility of particular "muscle groups." Your results will help you focus your work as you complete this workbook.

This 40-question assessment should take you no more than 20 minutes. Answer each question relatively rapidly. Rather than search for the "right" answer, simply choose the first response that represents how you see the situation at this moment. You will likely find more than one answer to be a good choice. *Choose only one for each question* — the one that would be your choice in most situations.

As you build your facilitation skills we encourage you to visit us at www.facilitator.org. Tell us how you are progressing. Share some stories with your fellow facilitators. You can even complete the Facilitation Skills Self-Assessment instrument again. Readers of our first book, *Managers as Facilitators*, have made several valuable contributions to building our online resource. We welcome you to do the same.

Facilitation Skills Self-Assessment

1. Facilitators should do the following with their personal beliefs when facilitating:
    a) Recognize that their beliefs may be different from those of group members
    b) Suspend all personal beliefs while facilitating and operate from the belief system of the group
    c) Use understanding of interaction of beliefs to choose interventions
    d) Understand that their personal beliefs will affect their facilitation
    e) Draw on understanding of personal beliefs as a benchmark when observing groups

2. Facilitators should consider the following when dealing with new groups or groups that have recently experienced significant changes:
    a) There is specific work required to be completed during different stages of group development before groups can progress to the next stage
    b) The only work a group has to do is the specific task it was assigned and any other activities should be excluded
    c) How a group progresses through the stages of group development affects the ways it is able to address its work
    d) Group members must learn about each other and how they will work together before they can be most successful
    e) Facilitators need to accept the fact that some groups are able to work together more easily than others

3. The most important and impactful thing a facilitator does is:
    a) Help a group run effective meetings
    b) Help a group clarify its task and keep it central to its activities
    c) Help people get along with each other
    d) Keep a group moving quickly through its meeting agenda
    e) Help people be clear about what they are trying to accomplish

4. If a group member complains about a fellow employee who, you believe, is interfering with the group's ability to complete its work, you:
    a) Know that one or more people can interfere with a group's ability to complete its work
    b) Share your own experiences and feelings about that employee
    c) Acknowledge the group member's feelings and help her or him decide how to help the group address the situation
    d) Acknowledge the group member's feelings and then, using the role of facilitator, decide how best to fix this problem
    e) Acknowledge the group member's feelings and then help him or her identify his or her options

5. Facilitators should consider the following impact regarding their own beliefs about the nature of conflict:
    a) Recognize that conflict has been studied and there are ways to systematically explore a conflict's dynamics
    b) Recognize that conflict is inevitable in groups and learn to live with it
    c) Recognize that conflict is one of the most challenging parts of facilitating groups
    d) Recognize that conflict, while it can be very exciting, hinders a group being able to work effectively together
    e) Recognize that conflict can be utilized as a positive for group productivity, when it is understood and used in a systematic way

6. Facilitators should help groups respond to their differences in the following ways:
    a) Help group members recognize how the differences affect how they work together
    b) Help group members better understand how the differences can help the group become more effective
    c) Help group members behave more consistently like one another
    d) Help group members use their understanding of differences when choosing how to work together
    e) Help group members develop systematic ways of understanding differences when they observe interactions within the group

7. In facilitation situations you use information about the group's history to:
   a) Choose interventions based upon your knowledge of the group's past
   b) Gather information about a group's history in a systematic and comprehensive way
   c) Focus on the interactions of the group today since that is so much more important than what happened in the past
   d) Identify patterns of behavior that are well established in the group
   e) Recognize that the behavior of a group today is closely tied to what has happened to the group in the past

8. To help a group reach consensus it is important for facilitators to:
   a) Give everyone who wants to a chance to express their point of view
   b) Ask quieter members of the group to speak up so that all opinions are heard
   c) Ask people with dissenting opinions to explain what has to change in order for them to support the group's decision
   d) Ask members to support the group's decision both within and outside the group
   e) Get the group to agree that consensus is necessary

9. When conflict arises during an organization change it is usually caused by:
   a) People not supporting, and sometimes even undermining, the change
   b) People being uncertain about how to interpret the change and what to do about it
   c) People being in different stages of change at the same time and not realizing it
   d) People taking a long time to get through the Goodbye stage of change
   e) People being well into the Hello stage when others are hearing about the change for the first time

10. During a group meeting a member complains about people or events outside of the group. As a facilitator you:
    a) Quickly make it clear that such off-topic conversations are unacceptable now and in the future
    b) Acknowledge the group member's strong feelings and how they are affecting the group and then help the group decide how it wishes to respond to the situation
    c) Politely but firmly inform the group member that he or she is off topic and needs to stay on task
    d) Recognize the impact that strong feelings can have on both the individual sharing and the larger group and how that can be distracting from the task at hand
    e) Acknowledge the group member's strong feelings and that the situation is affecting how the group member can participate in the group and then guide discussion back to topic

11. Facilitators should consider the following when examining their own experiences with conflict:
    a) Utilize a conflict model to better understand how they typically handle conflict situations
    b) Use a systematic understanding of how they and others respond to conflict in order to decide what action to take with the group
    c) Recognize that they use similar techniques for dealing with conflict in groups as they do in other parts of their lives
    d) Accept that their own experiences with conflict color how they approach conflict situations in groups
    e) Carefully remember how conflict has been difficult, even painful, and how things were better when there was no conflict

12. In facilitation situations you use personality and style differences in the following ways:
    a) Understand that there are systematic ways that have been used to categorize these differences
    b) See the differences as problems that must be minimized if the group is to be effective
    c) Use one of the systematic ways of categorizing personality or style differences as a foundation for understanding and acting
    d) Draw on a systematic way of categorizing personality or style differences as a benchmark when observing groups
    e) Recognize how differences among people affect the ways group members work together

13. Facilitators should consider the following when exploring traps groups can fall into regarding conflict:
    a) The biggest trap is letting a conflict get out of the control of the facilitator
    b) Draw on behavioral models to better understand the interactions among group members
    c) Some people and groups have patterns of getting into and staying in conflict
    d) Examine a conflict situation using a behavioral model to choose the intervention that will help the group move forward
    e) Accept that facilitators can have some positive impact on the ways groups deal with conflict

14. Facilitators should consider the following about the ways groups can deal with conflict:
    a) Recognize conflicts as they appear and help steer the group onto a more productive path
    b) Groups must avoid conflict or they will be less productive and have more angry group members
    c) Base intervention choices on the understanding of a conflict situation gained from systematically applying a behavioral model
    d) Refer to one of the behavioral models to better understand how a group successfully resolves a conflict
    e) Accept that when people get together and work at something, conflicts will arise

15. When you are going to lunch with a group you are facilitating, you:
    a) Focus your attention on the meal and service, avoiding conversation about the work session
    b) Ask how people are experiencing the work session, listen to the answers, and then identify what you have learned about the group
    c) Pay attention to what's said and participate in the conversation to learn more
    d) Listen to what people are saying
    e) Entertain the group with several stories

16. When someone talks nonstop during a session you are facilitating, you:
    a) Ask questions at an appropriate time in an attempt to help the person focus
    b) Interrupt the person at the first opportunity and make it clear that they are not to take over the meeting again
    c) Try to be patient and understand what you are being told
    d) Listen respectfully until the person runs out of things to say
    e) After listening carefully, help this individual and the group explore how the nonstop talking is affecting the group

17. Facilitators should respond to their own personality type or work-style preferences in the following way when facilitating:
    a) Match their own behaviors to the dominant personality typology or work-style preferences of the group
    b) Draw on understanding of a system of personality typology or work-style preferences as a benchmark when observing groups
    c) Use their personality or style in spite of pressure from groups to act differently
    d) Use understanding of a system of personality typology or work-style preferences when choosing interventions
    e) Understand how their personality or style impacts their interaction with groups

18. If someone is critical of your facilitation, you:
    a) Try not to react or get upset
    b) Automatically become curious and attempt to learn more
    c) Listen attentively and then explain your position
    d) Ask them why
    e) Try to understand why they feel the way they do and, if you agree, make some adjustments

19. You are having a very busy day and someone tells you to change the way you are completing a task. You believe the person is wrong, so you:
    a) Thank her or him for the input and keep doing what you were doing
    b) Explain that you are very busy, and that it is difficult for you to listen when you are feeling so much pressure
    c) Try to find out why she or he thinks you should change
    d) Acknowledge that the other way may be right, tell her or him you are very busy, and agree to follow up later
    e) Listen to her or his ideas, agree to briefly discuss things a little further, and commit to following up if you both agree that would be helpful

20. When you are ready to add your ideas, suggestions, or comments to a group discussion, as a facilitator you should:
    a) Often find it necessary to interrupt to ensure your points are not lost
    b) Make sure that everyone knows that when you speak everyone else should be quiet and listen only to you
    c) Check to see that everyone else has contributed their points before adding yours
    d) Look for a suitable break in the conversation and then interject your points
    e) Actively draw all group members into sharing their points before adding yours

21. When helping a group plan a project you should:
    a) Be clear about the roles that people will play to reduce the likelihood of interpersonal problems
    b) Help them develop a common understanding of the purpose of the project
    c) Complete the planning process rapidly to avoid the problem of "analysis paralysis"
    d) Help the group set clear goals
    e) Support the use of a project planning methodology

22. A group member comes to you outside of a group meeting and tells you about being upset by actions of other group members. As a facilitator you:
    a) Assure this group member that things are probably not as bad as they seem and everything is probably okay
    b) Quickly tell the group member that such information should not be shared with you
    c) Reflect back to this group member what you have heard and assist in helping him or her decide what to do next
    d) Make sure that this group member knows you understand how upset he or she is about this situation
    e) Reflect back to this group member what you have heard and help him or her decide how best to address it with the group

23. Facilitators should consider the following about the ways group members work together:
    a) Use understanding gained from using behavioral or psychological models in choosing what are priorities for improving performance
    b) Understand that support from the facilitator makes it easier for the group members to work together more effectively
    c) Draw on behavioral or psychological models for better understanding of the dynamics observed in group member interaction
    d) Recognize that there are degrees to which group members will work together
    e) Group members must work together because they are all in the group

24. A useful way for facilitators to think about conflict is that:
    a) It is an inevitable and uncomfortable result of working with people
    b) It is necessary for healthy groups but must be managed well
    c) It is simply unresolved differences and a normal occurrence
    d) It scares some people
    e) It need not be an unpleasant or difficult experience

25. Facilitation is best described as:
    a) A set of tools that helps people organize their work and make decisions
    b) A skill set that helps groups improve their work environment
    c) A process for helping people get their work done and improve the way they work together
    d) A method for helping people focus on their task
    e) A set of skills to be used when a third party is required

26. A facilitator should use projection in the following ways:
    a) Draw on the facilitator's understanding of what is occurring for him- or herself to make assumptions about what is true for others
    b) Recognize that what is true for him or her may be true for others
    c) Understand that what is true for him or her may often be true for others
    d) Facilitators should rarely assume that what is true for them is true for anyone else
    e) Check out with the group whether what is true for the facilitator is also true for the group

27. After you become involved in a big argument in a group meeting, as facilitator you:
    a) Act to be a quieter voice that encourages the group to settle down and begin discussing rather than arguing
    b) Experience the amazing changes a group can go through, working well one minute and arguing loudly the next
    c) Make decisions about what you can do to keep arguments from breaking out in the group
    d) Acknowledge the argument and invite the group to participate with you in resolving the conflict
    e) Recognize what happened and decide how you can avoid being drawn into group arguments in the future

28. When facilitating a group decision-making process you should:
    a) Help the group clearly define what decision it is going to make and what criteria it will use to make it
    b) Encourage the group to consider all points of view before making its decision
    c) Set a time-frame within which the decision will be made
    d) Consider who might be affected by the group's decision
    e) Help the group understand the decision-making process it will use

29. When facilitating a change process with a group it is important to remember that:
    a) People experience change in different ways
    b) People can move more rapidly from denying a change to accepting it if they are supported in that process
    c) People who resist the change need to be convinced to modify their position
    d) People often experience change as difficult and disturbing
    e) People accept change at their own pace

30. Facilitators can help groups run effective meetings by:
    a) Asking the group to avoid side conversations
    b) Convincing them to hold fewer meetings
    c) Distributing an agenda in advance of the meeting
    d) Restating the purpose of the meeting at its beginning and sticking to the agenda
    e) Evaluating the effectiveness of their meetings

31. Facilitators should consider the following dynamics when facilitating:
    a) Recognize some of the patterns in the ways that group members interact with other group members as well as what they expect from each other
    b) Focus on quickly getting to the tasks assigned and getting them done
    c) Utilize one or more behavioral models for better understanding the observed dynamics of groups
    d) Make choices for interventions based on the understanding gained from using behavioral models to understand a group
    e) Accept that groups are more than a simple collection of individuals and that they have unique dynamics

32. Focusing on the task is central to good facilitation because:
    a) Getting the work done is more important than anything else
    b) Putting the work first makes it easier to discuss ways to improve how people are working together
    c) People-related issues are becoming less important as organizations strive to become more productive
    d) Dealing with productivity problems that are related to interpersonal issues is most effectively done in the context of the work
    e) It helps people stay productive even if they have to deal with issues that are not directly related to the task at hand

33. People need to learn the role of facilitator because:
    a) It is replacing the role of manager in organizations
    b) More and more work is being done in teams
    c) Effective facilitators help improve both productivity and interdependence
    d) Effective facilitators help people cope with the pace and extent of change that exists in the modern workplace
    e) The workplace is becoming more diverse and effective facilitators help people who have different backgrounds work together more effectively

34. A group's assignment is clear when:
    a) There are defined goals that make sense to all group members
    b) The group has a common understanding of what it will look like when the assignment is successfully completed
    c) The leader who makes the assignment has communicated his or her expectations in writing
    d) There is a realistic deadline that has been clearly communicated
    e) Roles and responsibilities are clearly understood and group members are held accountable for completing tasks

35. Facilitators can help a group finish its work by:
    a) Encouraging the group to stick to its plan
    b) Asking the group to describe success and then work towards it
    c) Knowing when the group can declare that the work has been completed
    d) Pushing the group to stay on time
    e) Helping the group discover past successes

36. Facilitators should consider the following about types of groups:
    a) Recognize that some groups appear better matched to their assigned tasks than others
    b) There are two types of groups: those that complete their work successfully and those that don't
    c) Use what has been learned about a group, based on an accepted model, when choosing action to help it become more effective
    d) Accept that groups can learn to work together more effectively if they are given the proper help
    e) Assess groups based on an accepted model of group development

37. Facilitators can help people cope with major changes in the workplace by:
    a) Helping people learn how they can use past successes with change to deal with new ones
    b) Explaining that change is inevitable and is something that they will have to deal with
    c) Working with them to understand how the change will affect their work
    d) Supporting people to consciously address the feelings and concerns that arise as they work their way through the change process
    e) Getting people to talk about what the change means to them

38. When helping a group resolve a conflict it is important to remember that:
    a) Conflict is a part of every healthy group's experience and, if handled well, can lead to a more productive group
    b) Conflict should be stopped quickly or it will lead to more serious problems
    c) Conflict is difficult to contain and may cause group members to strongly dislike each other
    d) Conflict is challenging for both the group and the facilitator to handle well
    e) Conflict is a normal group experience during which a full expression of the differences can lead to resolution

39. Facilitators should refer in the following way to their own experiences with groups when facilitating:
    a) Use understanding gained from past experiences to choose interventions
    b) Understand that facilitators' experiences with groups will affect their perception of all aspects of the group
    c) Draw on their own experiences as a reference point when observing groups
    d) Recognize that each group member has his or her own experiences with groups
    e) Ignore their past experiences so they can take a fresh perspective with this group

40. As a facilitator, if a group member challenges your suggestion for the next step for the group, your best response would be:
    a) Since you know best what to do next, move right into doing your suggestion
    b) Strive to become curious, learn as much as you can about the opposing position, and be willing to modify your position based on new useful information
    c) Become curious about the challenge, recognize that it might simply be an alternative suggestion or an indication that there are more complex dynamics to uncover
    d) Continue to repeat your position in a firm but even manner
    e) Ask the challenging group member to explain more about why he or she is not agreeing with your suggestion

Score Sheet

For each question on the assessment, record your response in the appropriate place below. Each response is assigned 10, 7, 4, 2, or 0 points as indicated. Once all of your responses are recorded below, complete the following:

1. Find the items identified with the letter "T" in the left-hand column.
2. Add up the number of points associated with your choices with all of the T items. Record this number in the Scoring Assessment Table on the next page.
3. Continue this process for the S, G, C, P, L and H items.
4. Use the scoring guidelines to interpret your results

Element	Question	Points ->	10	7	4	2	0
S	1		c___	e___	d___	a___	b___
G	2		a___	c___	d___	e___	b___
T	3		b___	e___	c___	a___	d___
L	4		c___	e___	d___	a___	b___
G	5		e ___	a___	c___	b___	d___
G	6		d___	e___	b___	a___	c___
G	7		a___	b___	d___	c___	e___
P	8		c ___	d___	a___	e___	b___
H	9		c___	e___	b___	d___	a___
L	10		b___	e___	d___	c___	a___
C	11		b___	a___	c___	d___	e___
S	12		c___	e___	a___	d___	b___
G	13		d___	b___	a___	c___	e___
C	14		c___	e___	a___	d___	b___
L	15		b___	c___	d___	a___	e___
L	16		e___	e___	c___	d___	b___
S	17		d___	b___	a___	c___	e___
C	18		b___	e___	d___	a___	c___
C	19		c___	e___	d___	b___	a___
L	20		e___	c___	d___	a___	b___
P	21		b___	d___	a___	e___	c___
L	22		e___	c___	d___	a___	b___
G	23		a___	c___	b___	d___	e___
C	24		b___	c___	e___	d___	a___
ALL	25		c___	d___	b___	a___	e___
S	26		e___	a___	c___	b___	d___
C	27		d___	a___	e___	b___	c___
P	28		a___	e___	d___	c___	b___
H	29		b___	e___	a___	d___	c___
P	30		d___	c___	e___	a___	b___

G	31	d___	c___	a___	e___	b___
T	32	d___	b___	a___	e___	c___
ALL	33	c___	d___	e___	b___	a___
T	34	b___	e___	a___	d___	c___
P	35	c___	b___	e___	a___	d___
G	36	c___	e___	d___	a___	b___
H	37	d___	a___	c___	e___	b___
C	38	a___	e___	d___	c___	b___
S	39	a___	c___	b___	d___	e___
L	40	c___	b___	e___	d___	a___

Total ->

Scoring Assessment Table

The Facilitation Skills Self-Assessment will help you understand your abilities as they relate to the following elements:

- **Task** — your ability to help the group understand and focus on the work it has to do
- **Self** — your knowledge and understanding of yourself and others, and how you use this information to facilitate effectively
- **Group** — your ability to understand normal group behavior and how you use that information to support successful group work
- **Conflict** — your understanding of and ability to help groups work through conflict
- **Process** — your knowledge of planning, decision making, problem solving, and finishing work
- **Listening** — your ability to actively listen in facilitation situations
- **Change** — your understanding of and ability to help the groups manage change

Add up your points and enter the totals in the table below

Total points on the T lines: _____ Questions related to **TASK**
Total points on the S lines: _____ Questions related to **SELF**
Total points on the G lines: _____ Questions related to **GROUP**
Total points on the C lines: _____ Questions related to **CONFLICT**
Total points on the P lines: _____ Questions related to **PROCESS**
Total points on the L lines: _____ Questions related to **LISTENING**
Total points on the H lines: _____ Questions related to **CHANGE**

Points Grand Total: _____

Overall   your overall facilitation skill and knowledge level

My Overall Score _____

  0–30%   0 – 120 Need significant additional work and coaching before
                             facilitating
31–45%   121 – 180 Need some additional work and coaching before
                             facilitating
46–60%   181 – 240 Some general knowledge of working with people
61–78%   241 – 310 Good specific knowledge/experience with facilitation
79–93%   311 – 370 Skilled knowledge/experience with facilitation
94–100% 371 – 400 Expert knowledge/experience with facilitation

Task   your ability to help the group understand and focus on the work it has
          to do

My T Score _____

       0 – 25   Good general knowledge of working with people
     26 – 35   Some specific knowledge/experience with facilitation
     36 – 42   Intermediate knowledge/experience with facilitation
     43 – 50   Expert knowledge/experience with facilitation

Self   your knowledge and understanding of yourself and others, and how
          you use this information to facilitate effectively

My S Score _____

       0 – 35   Good general knowledge of working with people
     36 – 48   Some specific knowledge/experience with facilitation
     49 – 59   Intermediate knowledge/experience with facilitation
     60 – 70   Expert knowledge/experience with facilitation

Group   your ability to understand normal group behavior and how you
              use that information to support successful group work

My G Score _____

    0 – 50   Good general knowledge of working with people
    51 – 70   Some specific knowledge/experience with facilitation
    71 – 85   Intermediate knowledge/experience with facilitation
    86 – 100   Expert knowledge/experience with facilitation

Conflict your understanding of and ability to help groups work through
              conflict

My C Score _____

    0 – 45   Good general knowledge of working with people
    46 – 62   Some specific knowledge/experience with facilitation
    63 – 80   Intermediate knowledge/experience with facilitation
    81 – 90   Expert knowledge/experience with facilitation

Process   your knowledge of planning, decision making, problem solving,
              and finishing work

My P Score _____

    0 – 40   Good general knowledge of working with people
    41 – 55   Some specific knowledge/experience with facilitation
    56 – 71   Intermediate knowledge/experience with facilitation
    72 – 80   Expert knowledge/experience with facilitation

Listening your ability to actively listen in facilitation situations

My L Score _____

    0 – 45   Good general knowledge of working with people
    46 – 62   Some specific knowledge/experience with facilitation
    63 – 80   Intermediate knowledge/experience with facilitation
    81 – 90   Expert knowledge/experience with facilitation

Change your understanding of and ability to help groups manage change

My H Score _____

     0 – 25   Good general knowledge of working with people
26 – 35   Some specific knowledge/experience with facilitation
36 – 42   Intermediate knowledge/experience with facilitation
43 – 50   Expert knowledge/experience with facilitation

Unit 1
Facilitator: The Important New Role for Leaders and Managers

Warm-up

Facilitator is the most important role to emerge in the modern workplace. This is true because the workplace is changing as never before and effective facilitators are able to help individuals, groups, and entire organizations adapt and thrive in the face of these changes. Skilled facilitators help groups improve the quality and quantity of their work by working together more effectively. Leaders and managers have found that mastering the role of facilitator has helped them respond successfully to the changes happening around them and create the changes they want.

Facilitator is a distinct role, not just a set of skills. This mindset is important if you want to have the most positive impact for yourself and your organization. The key to developing a strong sense of the role of facilitator is understanding its very definition. In addition, you need to compare and contrast the role of facilitator with two other roles: leader and manager.

In some cases it is helpful to facilitate on an informal basis, rather than assuming a formally declared facilitation role. We call this informal approach *facilitating from the side.* Throughout this workbook, you will be asked to facilitate in different situations. Sometimes you will be more effective if you do so on an informal basis. In either case, you will be using the role of facilitator to help people.

In this unit you will develop your understanding of the role of facilitator by completing the following work-outs:

1.1 Learn the definition of facilitation: a process in which a person helps others to complete their work and improve the way they work together.

1.2 Learn the differences among the three roles of leader, manager, and facilitator. Determine the different situations in which each of the roles will work best.

1.3 Commit to memory the facilitation model and understand the importance of each of the model's four elements.

Work-out 1.1 - The definition of facilitation

Preparation

Your first facilitation work-out explores the very definition of facilitation: **a process in which a person helps others to complete their work and improve the way they work together**. We arrived at this definition in part by comparing and contrasting different experiences with facilitation — both our own and those of others.

One of the most common complaints we hear about "bad" facilitation experiences is the failure of the facilitator to keep the focus on the group's work. Other complaints include the facilitator having a hidden agenda or failing to listen. These negative experiences leave people with the feeling that using a facilitator is a waste of time.

Effective facilitation starts with a focus on the work that brings people together in the first place. It is a given that personalities and behaviors create challenges and difficulties for people. By focusing on the work, effective facilitators help people explore and understand these differences in a much less charged atmosphere. In fact, the focus on work makes it possible to delve more deeply into how people are working together — not because it "feels good" but because it is productive.

That is why the definition of facilitation includes both the work itself and how people work together. It is important that you integrate both of these concepts into your working definition of facilitation.

Examples of specific actions a facilitator takes to help people complete their work include:

- Planning meetings
- Clarifying tasks by asking questions
- Planning projects
- Making decisions
- Making sense of piles of information using various sorting and prioritization tools
- Identifying next steps
- Finishing work (coming to closure)

Examples of specific actions a facilitator takes to help people improve the way they work together include:

- Modeling desired behavior
- Helping a group resolve a conflict by using the conflict resolution process defined in Unit 5
- Helping a group recognize differences in members' work styles as assets that they can use, rather than obstacles to working together smoothly
- Influencing a group to talk about their differences in the context of their task
- Using the active listening methods described in Unit 7
- Helping a group determine if they are behaving competitively versus collaboratively

The actions cited above point out the two key aspects of effective facilitation: **helping others complete their work and improve the way they work together**. They provide methods to support both accomplishing tasks *and* attending to the way individuals work together. While any given situation may emphasize one aspect more heavily than the other, facilitators help people pay attention to both things in the long run. Facilitators help people make the connection between the quality of their work and the way they treat each other as they work together.

Exercise 1.1.1 — Your experiences with facilitation

Many people have had a wide range of experiences in their work with facilitators. Some people report extreme frustration with facilitators who fail to help a group complete their work. Others describe the work of effective facilitators as being almost "magical." Still others are neutral, expressing neither dissatisfaction nor awe. In this exercise we want you to recall your facilitation encounters and contrast either end of the spectrum, both your "good" and "bad" experiences.

Describe a "good" facilitation experience. _____

_____

_____

What made this a good experience? _____

_____

_____

How did the facilitator support the group's achieving its desired outcome? _____

_____

_____

What tools and techniques did this facilitator use?

_____

_____

_____

Describe the facilitator's behavior toward the group.

_____

_____

_____

Describe a "bad" facilitation experience. _____

_____

_____   _____

What made this a bad experience? _____

_____

_____

How did the facilitator interfere with the group's achieving its desired outcome? _____

_____

_____

What tools and techniques did this facilitator use?

_____

_____

_____

Describe the facilitator's behavior toward the group.

_____

_____

_____

What changes in approach or technique would you recommend to this facilitator? _____

_____

_____

What did you learn about facilitation as a result of this experience?

_____

_____

Work-out 1.2 - The differences among the roles of leader, manager, and facilitator

Preparation

Leaders and managers who are skilled facilitators have been very successful. Those people who attempt to use the old "direct-and-control" model of working with others are getting buried or passed over. Effective facilitators use their knowledge of organizational change to help others deal with its many facets. They have been able to help people focus on their work, and set clear goals and achieve them. **Helping focus attention on a few well-defined goals is extremely valuable to people who feel as if the very ground is shifting beneath them**. People who are skilled facilitators provide a calming influence *and* practical methods to be productive in the face of rapid change.

Facilitator is truly an equal and distinct role from leader and manager. Approaching facilitation as a distinct role instead of as a subset of management skills is critical to using facilitation well. The things people do using the facilitator role are sometimes in direct conflict with what they would do using either the traditional "direct and control" manager role or the "big picture" leader role. If individuals fail to be clear about the role they are using in a situation, others will be confused.

The table below provides a quick comparison of these three distinct roles. Most people who have a managerial title have to use all three roles to do their work. **It is challenging to integrate the roles of leader, manager, and facilitator because the roles themselves sometimes conflict, both in subtle and profound ways**. Study the table and become familiar with the differences among the three roles.

How does a person actually move from role to role while working with a group? What is the best role for a given situation? People must consider three factors when choosing among the three roles:

- The nature of the task at hand
- The degree of support needed from others in the organization
- The stage of the work group's development

Managers must first look at the nature of the tasks for which they are responsible. If the task is setting direction for a group, helping them see the bigger picture, then the leader role would be best. If the task is setting limits on the work, delegating, or defining deadlines, then the manager role would be the best choice. If the task is more complex, requiring the assistance of a number of other people to complete it, then the facilitator role would be best.

Comparing the Roles of Leader, Manager, and Facilitator

Leader	*Manager*	*Facilitator*
Concerned with doing the right thing	Concerned with doing things right	Concerned with helping people do things
Takes the long-term view	Takes the short-term view	Helps people find a view and articulate it
Concentrates on what and why	Concentrates on how	Helps people concentrate and be clear in the here and now
Thinks in terms of innovation, development, and the future	Thinks in terms of administration, maintenance, and the present	Helps people think and communicate their thoughts
Sets the vision; the tone and direction	Sets the plan; the pace	Helps people make meaning of tone, direction, and function well at the required pace
Hopes others will respond and follow	Hopes others will complete their tasks	Hopes others will engage in the process
Appeals to hopes and dreams	Monitors boundaries and defines limits	Helps others make meaning of hopes and dreams; pushes appropriately on boundaries
Expects others to help realize a vision	Expects others to fulfill their mission or purpose	Helps others articulate a shared vision and common mission or purpose
Inspires innovation	Inspires stability	Helps people respond to things that are new and things that remain the same

The second factor to consider when choosing the role is the degree of support needed from others. The manager role carries with it authority which can automatically produce compliance with decisions. A supportive response to a decision by a manager might sound like this: "My boss decided that I should do this. It sounds reasonable, so I'm going to do what she asked." In many cases the degree of support coming from such compliance is sufficient to complete a task. During a work day filled with tens of decisions, people often appreciate being told what to do.

If the degree of support for an initiative must spread widely across the organization, then the leader role is best to use. Remember from the table above that the leader role is used to take the long-term view, set direction, and inspire innovation. The leader role is thus most useful for building support broadly.

When a deeper level of support is needed, then the facilitator role works best. A higher level of participation will create commitment, rather than compliance, to completing a task and creating a desired outcome. People will feel more ownership in something they help create. Using the facilitator role is the most efficient, effective, and practical way to build a strong degree of support.

The third factor to consider when choosing the roles of leader, manager, or facilitator is the stage of the group's development. Less developed groups need more direction from the leader role and control from the manager role. If group members are less experienced working in effective groups, they will be more productive if the individual in charge occasionally uses the manager role. More developed groups respond well to a person using the facilitator role. They have the skills and experience to work with less direction. They have a track record of success and know what to do. With this more developed group, the facilitator can leave the technical content of the work to the group and help them attend to how they are working together.

The manager role and leader role cannot be neglected. These roles are needed to a varying extent, regardless of the nature of the task, support needed from others, or stage of group development. Acting in the leader role, an individual sets or clarifies the desired outcomes of the group. The person using the manager role is ultimately accountable for the completion of tasks. He or she owns the outcomes and is therefore responsible for the work necessary to accomplish them. People using the leader role and manager role are therefore never neutral observers. They have a stake in the successful completion of tasks.

Exercise 1.2.1 - Your task inventory

Think of some work tasks that you are responsible for completing, either alone or with others. Record those tasks in the table below. Choose a variety of tasks, ranging from specific (aspects of a project or company procedure) to general (completion of major parts of a project). Once you have recorded these tasks in the table, indicate whether or not you have direct responsibility for completing the task or producing a result directly related to it. Then indicate which role you believe you should use to move the task to completion.

My tasks	Person directly responsible	Which role will work best? leader/manager/facilitator

Exercise 1.2.2 - Choosing the best role for the situation

Choose three tasks from the table in Exercise 1.2.1. — one associated with each of the three roles of leader, manager, and facilitator. Describe each situation in more detail. Does the task require cooperation from people outside of your work group? Is the task to be completed relatively quickly? Once you have described the task and situation, make a case for using the role you chose to use. Then, complete the actions you outline and describe what happens.

Task/situation description

_____

_____

Why is the *leader* role best to use for this task at this time?

_____

_____

What actions will you take, using the leader role, to complete this task?

_____

_____

What do you believe will happen when you take the actions above?

_____

_____

What happened when you took the actions above?

_____

_____

Task/situation description

_____

_____

_____

Why is the *manager* role best to use for this task at this time?

_____

_____

_____

What actions will you take, using the manager role, to complete this task?

_____

_____

_____

What do you believe will happen when you take the actions above?

_____

_____

_____

What happened when you took the actions above?

_____

_____

_____

Task/situation description

_____

_____

_____

Why is the *facilitator* role best to use for this task at this time?

_____

_____

_____

What actions will you take, using the facilitator role, to complete this task?

_____

_____

_____

What do you believe will happen when you take the actions above?

_____

_____

_____

What happened when you took the actions above?

_____

_____

_____

Work-out 1.3 - The facilitation model

Preparation

Our facilitation model provides the basis for successfully fulfilling the role of facilitator. It points out practical things to do every day to produce the results people want and need. The figure below shows the model we created to illustrate the critical elements of facilitation and how those elements relate.

Task is at the center of the model because helping people be clear about their task is the single most important and influential thing a facilitator does. Every action facilitators take should help groups move closer to completing their task. Facilitators constantly ask themselves, "Is this action going to help the group complete its task?"

Facilitation Model

PROCESS
Actions and tools that help
a group get its work done

TASK
The work the group is
trying to get done

SELF
Using yourself as an instrument

GROUP
Understanding group dynamics

The most powerful and useful tool facilitators bring into a situation is themselves. For this reason, **Self** is one of the elements of the model that creates the base. Facilitators must know themselves and how they impact their groups. They frequently ask themselves the question, "What do I think is going on here? How do I feel about what is happening at this moment?" Another important aspect of Self is understanding how people are alike and how they differ. While every individual is unique, there are work-style preferences which can be described and understood. Effective facilitators use this knowledge to help others consider their differences as assets which can be used to get their work done.

Group is the other element forming the base of the facilitation model. While groups have many unique dynamics, much of what happens in groups is predictable. Understanding these group dynamics is essential to using the role of facilitator to help people more effectively get their work done. Facilitators help people become aware of how they are functioning and take steps to improve. Underlying all of this is a continuing focus on task. Task makes it easier for people to talk about emotions and be supportive to one another. The normal emotional energy available to people becomes a practical asset to helping the work get done.

The fourth and final element of the facilitation model is **Process**. Facilitators use their knowledge of task, self, and group to decide which facilitation process to use with a group. Process is a set of actions or tools, an exercise, or an intervention that helps groups make progress towards their goals.

As you work your facilitation fitness program, you must exercise all four elements of the model. Just as a successful Olympic long-distance runner builds cardiovascular capacity, an efficient upper body, strong legs, and a winner's attitude, so should you build strength in each area of the facilitation model.

Exercise 1.3.1 - Working with the facilitation model

The facilitation model is most useful when you can easily visualize its four elements, know what is important about each element, and apply your knowledge. Answer the questions below to help you strengthen your understanding of the facilitation model.

What do you feel is most important about each element of the model?

Task _____

_____

_____

Self _____

_____

_____

Group _____

_____

_____

Process _____

_____

_____

How will you use the model to help you be a more effective facilitator?

_____

_____

_____

_____

Cool-down - My self-assessment and action plan

World-class athletes visualize success at least as often as they practice and compete. Part of their "cooling down" process involves helping the body relax and helping the mind learn lessons. You have just completed three work-outs that provide a strong start to developing your "facilitation muscles." Cool down by answering the self-assessment questions below. Then, make an action plan to both apply your learning and improve your mastery of the subject matter of this unit.

For each of the work-outs in this unit, rate your understanding of the subject matter:

Work-out topic	Mastered	Understood	Need more work
1.1 Definition of facilitation	A	B	C
1.2 Differences among leader, manager, and facilitator	A	B	C
1.3 Facilitation model	A	B	C

What in this unit did you find particularly helpful to improving your ability to use the role of facilitator effectively ?

_____

_____

_____

How will you use what you have learned from this unit?

_____

_____

_____

What do you need to learn more about? What steps will you take to do so?

_____

_____

_____

Unit 2
Develop a Focus on Task

Warm-up

We define task as the work a group needs to complete. The facilitator's first job is to know what task people want and need to complete. Tasks may be the overall group assignment, an intermediate action step, or further developing the group's ability to work together. Facilitators help groups define and complete these tasks. Only by knowing the task can a facilitator choose the most helpful, practical actions.

The task at hand must be clear to both the group and the facilitator. The process of clarifying the task will help people complete it more quickly because everyone will have a clearer idea of the desired outcome.

A key job of the facilitator, then, is to help a group develop the habit of *first* clarifying tasks prior to "diving in to the work." This is true for a simple meeting or a complex project. Equally important, a facilitator helps groups clarify their tasks *quickly*. A few clarifying questions can help people achieve the clarity they need in just a few minutes.

Clarifying and focusing on task is the very essence of effective facilitation. This unit will give you the opportunity to develop this very important capability, and then build upon it. In this unit you will complete the following work-outs:

2.1 Helping people be clear about their assignment, or Charge.
2.2 Developing a Charter: purpose, goals, roles, and procedures.
2.3 Facilitating closure, the completion of work.

Work-out 2.1 - Clarifying the Charge to a group

Preparation

One reason that people sometimes feel overwhelmed at work is that their day-to-day workload clouds their overall assignment. The tasks come at a rapid pace and it is easy to lose track. A group will be faced with several, perhaps hundreds, of tasks during its existence. The tasks will range in scale from defining the overall purpose of the group to completing a specific project goal. Regardless of the scale of the task, it is essential that people clearly understand what they are trying to achieve.

Charge is the group's overall assignment. The Charge describes what must be accomplished for the group's work to be declared successful. It also must be measurable or quantifiable in some manner. The Charge:

- Makes clear what is expected of the group
- Defines the scope of the work and results expected
- Outlines the obligations of the group to the organization

A group's Charge usually originates from a leader or manager who is one or more levels above that of the group leader. Too often groups accept their Charge at face value, assume that they know what is expected, and fail to verify their interpretation of their assignment. No wonder so many reorganizations and projects go poorly! Clarifying the Charge is the most critical stage of forming a new department or project team. And yet, too many groups fail to be rigorous at this stage. An effective facilitator can help prevent this problem.

If the group believes the Charge to be ambiguous or otherwise unclear, it has the responsibility to seek clarity about it. An effective facilitator should assist the group to clarify it. Helping the leader or manager compare the Charge to the organization's mission is a simple, fast way to clarify the Charge. Answering the following three questions will clarify the Charge:

1. **What are we expected to produce?**
2. **What will it look like when we are successful?**
3. **How does this Charge support the strategic plan of the organization?**

Exercise 2.1.1 - Clarifying the Charge

Understanding the Charge is essential to the success of every group, whether that group is an ongoing department or an ad-hoc project team. Facilitators can help people clearly understand the Charge by completing a simple process outlined below.

The process of clarifying the Charge is more important than the initial Charge statement itself because it leads to a clearer understanding of what is expected. It is faster to complete each step in the process with both the issuer of the Charge and the group present. To complete this exercise, help a group work through this process:

1. **Issuer of the Charge states the desired outcome.**
2. **Issuer and group identify measures that help define success or failure.**
3. **Group interprets Charge based upon 1 and 2 above.**
4. **Issuer and group complete any further discussion needed to develop a common understanding of the Charge.**

The issuer of the Charge answers the following questions:

What is this group expected to produce? _____

_____

_____

What will it look like when the group successfully completes this charge?

_____

_____

_____

What measures will help the group track progress and define success or failure? _____

_____

_____

The group and/or issuer of the Charge answer the following questions:

What measures will help the group track progress and define success or failure? _____

_____

_____

What changes are necessary to clarify the Charge? _____

_____

_____

_____

The group makes the following response to the Charge:

We believe that the Charge is: _____

_____

_____

_____

The group and issuer of the Charge agree on the final Charge statement and any relevent measures.

The Charge that has been agreed to is: _____

_____

_____

_____

Measures that indicate success or failure are: _____

_____

_____

_____

Work-out 2.2 - Charter: purpose, goals, roles, and procedures

Preparation

The Charge to a group serves as the basis for developing its Charter. A Charter consists of **purpose**, **goals**, **roles**, and **procedures**. A Charter can be scaled up to describe the work of an entire department or scaled down to fit a project plan. Each of the four elements of a Charter is described in the table below.

	Questions answered	How the element is used
Purpose	• What do we produce? • Who do we serve? • What difference will we make to our customers?	• Aid to planning, problem solving, and decision making. • Guide activities with internal and external customers.
Goals	• What do we need to do to fulfill our purpose? • When do we need to accomplish this goal? • Who will be responsible for this goal?	• Identify measures of success. • Establish group and individual accountability.
Roles	• Where do I fit in? • What capabilities do each of us bring to the group? • Do our roles make it possible to fulfill our purpose? • Does my role give me the opportunity to grow?	• Clarify how group members are interdependent. • Establish group and individual accountability. • Identify group and individual boundaries.
Procedures	• How will the group complete its work? • How will we get along? • How will we resolve conflicts?	• Set guidelines for behavior. • Support interdependence. • Support increased productivity.

Developing and using a Charter has a profound impact on a group's ability to complete its work and work together effectively. Although some time investment is required, most groups report that their Charter saves them time and money later. This is a big help when the pressure is on.

Exercise 2.2.1 - Helping a group define its purpose

Helping members develop a common understanding of their overall **purpose** is critical to creating a productive, supportive group that is capable of fulfilling its Charge. Once a clear Charge has been issued, a group can usually define its purpose in as little as one hour. This investment pays off later because the group's purpose will prove to be a powerful aid to decision making. Since groups make hundreds of decisions during their existence, this tool will be well used. A clear purpose statement answers the following questions:

1. **Why does this group exist?**
2. **Who do we serve? Who are our customers?**
3. **What difference can our group make?**
4. **How does this group's work support the mission of the organization?**

In this exercise we want you to help a group develop a purpose statement. It should be approximately 25 words in length. Have people begin by recording their answers to the series of questions below. Have them do so individually, in silence. Then, help them work as a group to combine the answers into one or two sentences that decribe the purpose of the group.

What do I believe is the reason this team exists? _____

_____

_____

_____

Who are the primary customers of my team's work? _____

_____

_____

_____

When my group does its job well, what difference does it make to its customers and the organization? _____

_____

_____

_____

After hearing individuals' answers to the above questions, have them identify common themes that have emerged. Record them in "bullet" form on a flip-chart, as well as below. _____

_____

_____

_____

Draft a purpose statement that uses the common themes generated by the group. _____

_____

_____

_____

If necessary, help the group use a consensus process to come to agreement. The consensus process is dealt with in detail in Unit 6. The series of questions to be answered in order to reach consensus are as follows:

1. **Can you live with this decision?**
2. **Will you support it within the group?**
3. **Will you support it outside of the group?**

If one or more persons answers "no" to one of these questions, they must then answer the fourth question:

4. **What has to change in order for you to support this?**

Exercise 2.2.2 - Setting goals

Once a group develops a purpose that is commonly understood by all, members have to set goals in order to achieve their purpose. **Goals** define the work that must be done, translating the purpose into specific accomplishments. Goals make it possible for groups to determine how they are progressing and ultimately whether they have fulfilled their purpose. Every goal should have some measure that will make it clear when the goal is accomplished. An effective format for setting goals is:

- **What** exactly should be done?
- **Who** will be accountable for the completion of this goal?
- **When** must the goal be accomplished?

An excellent test of whether or not a goal is specific enough is to apply the criteria defined by the "SMART" acronym. Goals that meet the SMART criteria have proven to be useful to groups. SMART stands for:

S pecific .... Know exactly what needs to be done.

M easurable .... How will you know whether it is done?

A ttainable/Achievable ... Can it really be done? Be reasonable in the stretch.

R ealistic .... Fits the responsibility and nature of the group.

T ime-bound .... Know when it needs be completed.

In this exercise we want you to help a group set goals that will enable it to achieve its purpose. Do so by helping members answer the questions on the following page.

What goals do we need to accomplish to fulfill our purpose? (Process tip: use brainstorming.) _____

_____

_____

_____

For each of the goals above, help the group apply the SMART criteria. Create several worksheets or several flip-charts using the format illustrated in the table below.

Goal:	
Specific	
Measurable	
Attainable	
Realistic	
Time-bound	

Conduct a "necessary and sufficient" test:

• Consider each goal one at a time. For each, answer the question, "Is this goal *necessary* to fulfill our purpose?" Discard any goal receiving a "no." (Process tip: use the consensus process on page 45.)

• Is the entire set of goals *sufficient* to achieve our purpose? If not, what goals must be added?

_____

_____

_____

_____

Exercise 2.2.3 - Helping individuals define their roles

Lack of clarity regarding roles is one of the most common causes of problems for groups. Cross-functional project teams, whose members report to functional managers outside of the team, are particularly susceptible to confusion around roles. People on these teams make assumptions about their duties and responsibilities without checking with others. In most of these teams, it is rare that people are assigned from every primary functional area of the organization. Therefore, people usually need to "wear more than one hat" in order for the team to succeed.

Thus, clearly defining roles for group members is essential to fulfilling the purpose of the group. There are a large number of acceptable formats to use for role or job descriptions. We recommend a simple four-part format:

1. **A simple, one-paragraph description of the person's primary duties, customers (internal and external), and functions**
2. **A "bullet list" of the person's primary activities**
3. **Special skills, knowledge, abilities, and experiences required**
4. **Specific goals for which this person is primarily accountable**

In this exercise we want you to help individuals in a group establish the roles necessary to fulfill its purpose. Create enough copies of the "Role Description Worksheet" for each member of the group. Help individuals complete their worksheets. You can do this one-on-one or in a group meeting. If conducting this exercise in a meeting, make sure people are given time to complete their worksheets alone, in silence.

Role Description Worksheet

Describe your role(s) in this group. _____

_____

_____

_____

Make a list of the primary activities you complete in support of the group.

_____

_____

_____

_____

What special skills, knowledge, abilities, and experiences do you feel are necessary for this role to be successfully fulfilled?

_____

_____

_____

_____

List below the group's goals for which you are responsible.

_____

_____

_____

_____

How does your role help your group fulfill its purpose? _____

_____

_____

Exercise 2.2.4 - Helping a group agree upon roles

Once everyone has completed his or her Role Description Worksheet the group needs to review and agree upon the results. Facilitate a discussion among group members to help them reach agreement about each role description. Work through the questions below for each role description.

Does anybody have any questions about this role description?

_____

_____

What changes, if any, are needed to clarify this role description?

_____

_____

Conduct a "necessary and sufficient" test:

•   **Consider each role one at a time. For each, answer the question, "Is this goal *necessary* to fulfill our purpose?" Discard any role receiving a "no." (Process tip: use the consensus process on page 45.)**

•   **Is the entire set of roles *sufficient* to achieve our purpose? If not, what roles must be added?**

_____

_____

_____

_____

Use a consensus process to help the group agree that the role descriptions have been completed satisfactorily.

Set a follow-up date to briefly update each role description and add or subtract roles as necessary.

Exercise 2.2.5 - Helping a group establish procedures

Many groups are tempted to stop their Charter development process after finalizing their purpose, goals, and roles. In these cases, groups assume (incorrectly) that standard procedures are already documented elsewhere. For example, the group might assume that the organization's employee handbook, published by human resources, already contains all the procedures they need. Failing to set up a few key procedures that are unique to the group's purpose is a major mistake for these groups.

Successful groups set up procedures to define how people will work together. Some procedures, such as ground rules for behavior, are oriented to group interdependence, a subject we cover in detail in Unit 4. It is true that some organizational procedures, such as filing expense reports and providing performance feedback, need not be replicated. Doing so would be a waste of time. But there are some key procedures that groups need to agree upon and use, if they are going to fulfill their purpose. These procedures are:

- Ground rules
- Meetings — scheduling and running them effectively
- Guidelines for using communication tools (voice mail, e-mail, etc.)
- Decision making
- Introducing a new group member
- Helping a group member leave smoothly

Ground rules are the procedures established most frequently by groups. Unfortunately, they are also the procedures that are most frequently ignored. This happens because many groups fail to include a mechanism for enforcing the ground rules themselves! In this exercise we want you to help a group set up its ground rules. You will facilitate a discussion using the outline on the next page, entitled Procedure Worksheet. You may also choose to help the group to set up other procedures using this same worksheet.

Procedure Worksheet

The name of this procedure is: _____

_____

This procedure will help us: _____

_____

_____

In the past, some of the worst experiences we have ever had because we did not have this procedure, or had it but failed to use it, include:

_____

_____

_____

The components and/or steps for this procedure are as follows:

_____

_____

_____

_____

When this procedure is working well, these things will be happening for the people in our group: _____

_____

_____

The situations or conditions under which this procedure will be used are:

_____

_____

_____

Work-out 2.3 - Closure: finishing work

Preparation

One of the joys people experience at work comes from completing a project. When they work hard, achieve their goal, and receive well-deserved recognition, people justifiably feel fulfilled. Closure is not always a positive experience, however. Sometimes, people fail. In these cases it is especially critical to help the individual or group learn the lessons and move on. Achieving closure, or "finishing work," is critical to every human being who works. It is often seen, felt, or otherwise experienced as:

- A culminating experience
- Learning something new
- A sense or expression of accomplishment
- Achieving a goal or objective, and getting recognized for it
- Failing to achieve a goal in time
- Turning attention to other matters

Closure helps avoid the accumulation of "unfinished business" which interferes with the ability to complete work. Unfinished business refers to any situation or work that is not complete, and that may cause one or more individuals to continually return to the work. Unfinished business will hold people's attention. If people accumulate too many tasks or situations for which they fail to achieve closure, they will become literally stuck or paralyzed from doing anything else.

If a group has not agreed, in an obvious and overt manner, that a topic, problem, or task is complete, some members will consider it complete while others will want to address it further. This difference will cause the group to lose focus.

Bringing a topic to closure does not mean that it can never be raised again. It means that the group has completed what it can do on the topic for the moment. Part of closure can be scheduling it for attention at some point in the future.

A group that achieves true closure is able to turn its attention and energy to other work. Tension around the issue or business at hand is reduced through the attainment of a goal, or agreement that no more effort will be extended in that direction.

Exercise 2.3.1 - Your experience of closure

In this exercise we want you to develop a strong, personal sense of closure.
Become familiar with your emotional response to achieving closure. Become
equally familiar with your response to tasks or situations that are not yet
complete.

**Think of a project or task you completed. How did you and the rest of your
group know that the work was done?** _____

_____

_____

**Think of a project or task you completed in a manner that was very
satisfying to you. Describe your emotional responses to completing this
work:**

_____

_____

_____

**Remembering the same project or task from above, how did other people
respond when the work was complete?** _____

_____

_____

**Think of a project or task you have not yet completed. Describe your
thoughts and emotions as you review this unfinished work.**

_____

_____

**Remembering the same project or task from above, how do other people
seem to be responding to this unfinished work?**

_____

_____

_____

Exercise 2.3.2 - Facilitating closure: helping a group finish its work

In this exercise we want you to help a group develop an understanding of the importance of closure and develop guidelines for achieving closure. After explaining the concept of closure, ask them the questions below.

Are there currently any tasks or situations that are unfinished? If so, what has been the impact on the group?

_____

_____

_____

_____

Are there currently any tasks or situations that have been completed to the satisfaction of all? What has that experience been like?

_____

_____

_____

_____

How will this group communicate the closure of tasks or situations? How will everyone know, and agree, that closure has been achieved?

_____

_____

_____

_____

What can you do in the role of facilitator to help a group experience closure? What are the practical actions you can take to help a group know that its work is really done? _____

_____

_____

_____

Cool-down - My self-assessment and action plan

You have completed three work-outs that are fundamental to your conditioning as a top-notch facilitator. Answer the self-assessment questions below. Then, make an action plan to both apply your learning and improve your mastery of the subject matter of this unit.

For each of the work-outs in this unit, rate your understanding of the subject matter:

Work-out topic	Mastered	Understood	Need more work
2.1 Clarifying the Charge to a group	A	B	C
2.2 Developing a Charter	A	B	C
2.3 Facilitating closure	A	B	C

What in this unit did you find particularly helpful to improving your ability to effectively use the role of facilitator?

_____

_____

_____

How will you use what you have learned from this unit?

_____

_____

_____

What do you need to learn more about? What steps will you take to do so?

_____

_____

_____

Unit 3
Using Yourself as an Instrument

Warm-up

As an effective facilitator, the most powerful tool you bring into a situation is yourself. To fulfill the role successfully, you must become more aware of how to **use yourself as an instrument** to help groups. Facilitation is not simply developing a plan for how you will interact with the group and then implementing it. Groups are not that static! They are fluid, constantly changing in subtle and dramatic ways. The emotional responses you observe are always different. To fulfill the role, facilitators must be flexible. Facilitators must constantly adjust what they expect, plan, and do. A key to this pliability is using yourself as an instrument. You use yourself to gain understanding of what is happening in the group at any moment, model the behaviors you desire the group to exhibit, and gain the group's cooperation in trying new approaches.

Using yourself as an instrument starts with the old adage, "know thyself." You must understand how your values, beliefs, needs, perspectives, experiences, and capabilities affect what you perceive to be occurring in your group. This knowledge of yourself enables you to consciously adjust your perceptions of a group based on known differences. Understanding yourself protects you from unconsciously using projections (assuming what is true for you is true for them) that are not helpful.

Facilitators continually modify their actions and recommendations based on their evolving perception of the group. Using yourself effectively as a "barometer" for the group, you can be more confident in the action you take, including calling attention to concerns and feelings (e.g., being bored, frustrated, or angry). Acknowledging those feelings enables people to take more productive directions, particularly if they maintain a focus on their tasks. In this unit, you will develop the ability to use yourself as an instrument by working with the following concepts:

3.1 Strengthen your sense of yourself by identifying your values, beliefs, needs, experiences, capabilities, and perspectives as they relate to facilitation.
3.2 Challenges with understanding your own work-style preferences and those of group members.
3.3 Challenges with working with people who have different styles.

Work-out 3.1 - Strengthening your sense of yourself

Preparation

Highly skilled facilitators know themselves very well and they constantly strive to know themselves better. As they gain more experience, effective facilitators find they have to do less for their groups to accomplish more. Their "minimalist" approach to intervention produces maximum results in large part because they know themselves so well. "Letting the group be the star" is one of the most important aspirations of effective facilitators.

In our busy lives we seldom stop to ask ourselves about our reasons or motivations for saying or doing things. To become an effective facilitator we *always* have to know why we are saying or doing things. We have found that evaluating our values, beliefs, needs, experiences, capabilities, and perspectives provides a strong foundation upon which to build our sense of ourselves. Each of these six elements of self-understanding is defined below.

- **Values:** what you consider to be important
- **Beliefs:** what you think is true — your reality
- **Needs:** what you require to sustain yourself
- **Experiences:** the events you have participated in or lived through
- **Capabilities:** what you can do well
- **Perspectives:** your mental viewpoints coming from the accumulation of your values, beliefs, needs, experiences, and capabilities

We often take our values and beliefs for granted. We become aware of them when confronted with an action that we experience as offensive or untrue. As human beings, we seek to get our needs met in a variety of ways. It is important to understand what needs you are attempting to get met in working as a facilitator. Each experience gives us a chance to improve our capability to facilitate. We gain perspective as we test our values, shape our beliefs, work to get our needs met, and develop new capabilities from our experiences.

Exercise 3.1.1 - Defining your values

Your personal values have a big impact on your ability to facilitate. **Values are defined as what you consider to be important**. In this exercise we want you to define your values that affect your facilitation. Look for values that may conflict with fulfilling the role of facilitator. Ask yourself if you are willing to adjust these values.

Your values inventory

Check one item from each pair below. Either choice can be helpful. Just be aware that your choices affect how you facilitate.

___ Completing tasks	or	___ Having good interactions.
___ Working in broad strokes	or	___ Making sure the details are right.
___ Getting everyone to participate	or	___ Getting work done quickly.
___ Avoiding conflict.............................	or	___ Facing conflict.
___ Working from a plan	or	___ Being spontaneous.
___ Responding to events	or	___ Managing what occurs.
___ Letting people be quiet	or	___ Insisting people speak.
___ Letting people be loud....................	or	___ Maintaining quieter atmosphere.
___ Tolerating disruptions.....................	or	___ Avoiding disruptions.
___ Focusing almost exclusively on work	or	___ Focusing almost exclusively on people.
___ Getting to solutions quickly	or	___ Learning more about the problem.
___ Following the group's rules	or	___ Bending rules wherever necessary.
___ Ignoring disrespectful behavior.....	or	___ Confronting disrespectful behavior.
___ Working for consensus	or	___ Agreeing to disagree.

Circle the three items above that reflect your most strongly held values.
Why are these values so strong for you? _____

_____

_____

_____

_____

How do you see these values affecting your facilitation of groups?

_____

_____

_____

_____

_____

What do you think of others whose values conflict with your own?

_____

_____

_____

_____

_____

What have you learned about yourself and your faciltiation by completing
this values exercise? _____

_____

_____

_____

_____

Exercise 3.1.2 - Defining your beliefs about facilitation

Our beliefs place limits on what we think is possible. Your beliefs thus have a huge impact on your ability to facilitate effectively. In this exercise we want you to define your beliefs that affect your facilitation. **Beliefs are defined as what you think is true — your reality**. They are most often based on or in alignment with our values. Look for beliefs that may conflict with fulfilling the role of facilitator. Ask yourself if you are willing to adjust these beliefs.

Your beliefs inventory about facilitation
Look at each of the following statements and decide whether it is true or false. Either choice can be helpful. Just be aware that your choices affect how you facilitate.

True (T) or False (F):

___T___ As a facilitator, I must do whatever is necessary to get the group to complete its work.
___T___ As a facilitator, I must keep control of group meetings.
___F___ As a facilitator, I must know what the group should do next.
___T___ As a facilitator, I must listen to every group member.
___T___ As a facilitator, I must be willing to let groups make mistakes.
___T___ As a facilitator, I must not let myself get bored with meetings.
___F___ As a facilitator, I must avoid expressing my opinion.
___T___ As a facilitator, I must be *the* expert on facilitation tools and processes.
_____ As a facilitator, I must provide feedback to the group and group members.
___T___ As a facilitator, I must focus on the task at hand.
___T___ As a facilitator, I must be an example in all that I do and say.

Circle the three items above that reflect your most strongly held beliefs. Why are these beliefs so strong for you? _____

_____

_____

_____

_____

How do you see these beliefs *helping* your facilitation of groups as you seek to help them be more effective?

_____

_____

_____

_____

_____

_____

How do you see these beliefs *hindering* your facilitation of groups as you seek to help them be more effective?

_____

_____

_____

_____

_____

_____

How do you respond to others whose beliefs are different from your own?

_____

_____

_____

_____

_____

_____

Exercise 3.1.3 - Defining your beliefs about groups

Your beliefs about groups will affect your ability to facilitate their work. In addition, beliefs that people have about their groups have a huge impact on their success or failure. If people believe they can succeed, they have a good chance of doing so. Conversely, if a group feels that it is working on a doomed project, it will most likely fail. In this exercise we want you to define your beliefs about groups.

Your beliefs inventory about groups
Look at each of the following statements and decide whether it is true or false. Either choice can be helpful. Just be aware that your choices affect how you facilitate.

True (T) or False (F):
___ Groups are usually the best way to accomplish tasks.
___ Groups are rarely the best way to accomplish tasks.
___ Groups take longer to complete tasks.
___ Groups complete tasks in a more creative and complete way.
___ Groups always have someone who wants to dominate.
___ Groups always have someone who wants to take credit for the group's success.
___ Groups have members who would rather socialize than get the work done.
___ Groups have members who are so focused on the task that they are hard to work with.
___ Groups who have worked together for a long time will not be open to new members.
___ Groups spend too much time on how they will work together and not enough time on their work.
___ Groups are too quick to get on with their task before they are clear on their work processes.
___ Groups should avoid conflict, if they are to be successful.

Circle the three items above that reflect your most strongly held beliefs. Why are these beliefs so strong for you? _____

_____

_____

_____

_____

How do you see these beliefs affecting your facilitation of groups?

_____

_____

_____

_____

_____

_____

How do you interpret others whose beliefs conflict with your own?

_____

_____

_____

_____

_____

_____

How do you interpret the results of your inventory?

_____

_____

_____

_____

_____

_____

Exercise 3.1.4 – Identifying your needs

Abraham Maslow identified five levels of needs experienced by nearly everyone. **We define needs as what you require to sustain yourself.** To varying degrees, facilitators and group members may seek to have these needs met through their participation in groups. Those levels are physiological (hunger, thirst, shelter, sex, and other bodily needs), safety (physical and emotional safety), social (affection, belongingness, acceptance, and friendship), esteem (self-respect, autonomy, achievement, status, and recognition), and self-actualization (to become what one is capable of becoming, growth, self-fulfillment). In this exercise please identify:

- How you get these needs met through facilitating groups
- How trying to get these needs met through facilitating may create problems

Need	How facilitation helps you meet this need	How trying to get this need met through facilitation may cause problems
Physiological	_____ _____ _____	_____ _____ _____
Safety	_____ _____ _____	_____ _____ _____
Social	_____ _____ _____	_____ _____ _____
Esteem	_____ _____ _____	_____ _____ _____
Self-actualization	_____ _____ _____	_____ _____ _____

Exercise 3.1.5 - Your experiences with facilitation

Some people have told us that a single experience with an effective facilitator got them keenly interested in facilitation. Others, however, experience the word facilitation itself as a negative trigger — it immediately brings about bad feelings from a past episode. In this exercise we want you to interpret some significant experiences you have had with facililtation and working in groups. We define experiences as **the events you have participated in or lived through**. Describe how these experiences could affect your facilitation.

Refer back to Exercise 1.1.1 on page 25, and recall your "good" experience with facilitation. How might this experience impact your facilitation?

_____

_____

_____

How does that experience affect your work with groups now?

_____

_____

_____

Refer back to Exercise 1.1.1 on page 26, and recall your "bad" experience with facilitation. How might this experience impact your facilitation?

_____

_____

_____

How does that experience affect your work with groups now?

_____

_____

_____

_____

Exercise 3.1.6 - Your capabilities as a facilitator

As you have no doubt determined, being an effective facilitator requires a considerable number of capabilities. In this exercise we want you to identify and describe the capabilities you already possess. **Capabilities are defined as what you can do well**. Brainstorm a list of your capabilities and complete the table below.

Capability	Difference it makes for your groups
Example: good at helping people reduce tension in the midst of conflict	Groups are more productive because their focus on task helps them deal with difficult behavior more successfully.

Exercise 3.1.7 - Your gaps as a facilitator

Given what you have learned so far about facilitation, you may perceive that there are some areas that you need to develop. In this exercise we want you to identify and describe the capabilities that you need to develop.

Capability I need to develop	How this gap limits my ability to facilitate
Example: working effectively with aggressive people	I might let an aggressive person take over a meeting when it is clear that a majority of the attendees want more opportunities to express themselves.

Exercise 3.1.8 - Your perspective on facilitation

Our perspective is that using groups is a great way to accomplish tasks and that the role of facilitator is vital to their success. It is important that groups stay on task, deal effectively with the normal difficulties that always arise when more than one human being attempts to accomplish some work together, and put in extra effort when necessary.

We strive to help the group "be the star" and take great satisfaction when it is successful. We put the group first, especially when accolades and rewards are given. During meetings, we support the group's creation of its own ideas. Facilitators we have trained know that work sessions with their groups are going well when group members are doing most of the talking. These facilitators ask well-timed questions that help group members contribute.

In this exercise we want you to describe your perspective on facilitation. Perspectives are defined as **your mental viewpoints coming from the accumulation of your values, beliefs, needs, experiences, and capabilities**.

Describe your general perspective on facilitating groups.

_____

_____

_____

_____

_____

What changes would you like to make in your facilitation perspective in order to be more effective in supporting groups to complete their work?

_____

_____

_____

_____

_____

Work-out 3.2 – Challenges with understanding differing styles

Preparation

An important way that facilitators know themselves better is to understand the ways they prefer working and interacting with others. These style differences have a significant effect on how facilitators approach particular situations and interpret the behavior of others. These approaches have been described in terms of work styles. Each person prefers one or more styles over alternative styles. This is a normal process.

There is no one "right" style. Some styles may be more effective in particular situations. People can develop the capacity to recognize their own preferences and choose to use alternative styles as the situation demands. Through the understanding of style preferences facilitators can make more conscious choices about the most effective styles to use in particular situations.

A very useful approach to identifying work-style differences is the INSIGHT Inventory®, developed by Patrick Handly and available through HRD Press. The model provides general descriptions of the preferences people exhibit — not detailed psychological assessments. These descriptions help us better appreciate and benefit from the normal differences that exist among people.

The INSIGHT Inventory describes people's preferences along four continuums: how they get their way (how people express their thoughts, present ideas, and assert themselves); how they respond to others (how people approach and respond to others, particularly groups of people); how they pace their activities (how quickly they take action and make decisions); and, how they deal with details (how they structure their time, carry out projects, and handle details). The figure below depicts these continuums and the opposites associated with each.

Indirect	**Getting Own Way**	Direct

Reserved	**Responding to People**	Outgoing

Urgent	**Pacing Activity**	Steady

Unstructured	**Dealing with Details**	Precise

Each of the preferences described on these continuums reflects a different way of operating and experiencing others. Each has strengths that can contribute positively when used appropriately. Each of these tendencies also has vulnerabilities that lead to less productive behavior, especially when a person is under stress. Experiencing higher levels of stress often leads to people overusing their preferred mode. Such overuse can lead to problems. It is helpful for facilitators to both learn about their own preferences and the types of situations where it might be good to operate from the other end of a particular continuum.

Understanding the preference choices requires learning about the various ways the preference can be expressed (what you might observe in your own behavior or the behavior of others), some of the inherent strengths of this preference, how a person with this preference will tend to act when under stress, the facilitation situations where the particular approach would be good to use, and the counterpoint, situations where this approach would be less productive.

Continuum: Getting Own Way

Preference: INDIRECT

    Expressed:
- Positions stated carefully and diplomatically
- Uses support and tact to influence others
- Acts in an approachable and tactful manner
- Prefers to negotiate rather than argue
- Tends to ask rather than tell
- Avoids overselling ideas

    Strength:
- Ability to keep own issues in the background
- Phrasing comments carefully to not offend or push own agenda

    Responses to stress
- May give in when not really in agreement
- May avoid when should confront
- Can become hesitant and unsure

Preference: DIRECT

    Expressed:
- States position on issues candidly and frankly
- Influences others with an assertive, direct approach
- Comes across as forceful and self-assured
- Prefers to confront conflicts and openly debate differences
- Tends to tell rather than ask
- Presents ideas with confidence, sometimes overstating them

    Strength:
- Taking charge, especially in situations that need control and clear direction
- Getting vague or hidden issues out on the table and restated in a frank, straightforward way

    Responses to stress
- Will fight back, sometimes prematurely
- Can get argumentative and blunt
- May become demanding and aggressive

Situations to use INDIRECT approach and to avoid DIRECT approach:
- Group is focused appropriately on task
- Group requires less guidance because it already works together very effectively

Situations to use DIRECT approach and to avoid INDIRECT approach:
- Group is unable to achieve a productive focus
- Group is disagreeing about how to proceed and requires more clear intervention

Continuum: Responding to People

Preference: RESERVED

    Expressed:
- Is most at ease interacting with others one on one
- Keeps emotions rather private and self-contained
- Gets energized when alone and away from activity
- Prefers to think problems through alone to clarify feelings
- Uses few gestures and facial expressions when talking
- Contacts friends and acquaintances occasionally

    Strength:
- Being a good listener and feeling comfortable with letting others talk more than self
- Holding information confidentially and not giving it away by expressing own emotions

Responses to stress
- May withdraw from people
- May be overly quiet and self-contained
- May keep thoughts to self when talking would be better

Preference: OUTGOING

    Expressed:
- At ease interacting with many people and groups
- Shares emotions openly and freely
- Gets energized by people contact and lots of activity
- Prefers to talk problems out with others to clarify feelings
- Uses lots of gestures and facial expressions when talking
- Contacts friends and acquaintances frequently

    Strength:
- Being good at meeting and greetings others, putting them at ease, and making them feel important
- Staying connected and up to date on personal issues that friends and business associates may be going through

Responses to stress   • May feel hurt and become emotionally reactive or
                              explosive
                            • May over talk or use words to fight
                            • May withhold their usual friendliness

Situations to use RESERVED approach and to avoid OUTGOING approach:
  • Group is well established and expectations of each person are clear
  • Group is skilled at managing interpersonal dynamics

Situations to use OUTGOING approach and to avoid RESERVED approach:
  • Group is new and roles are not yet established
  • Group has extensive interpersonal dynamics that negatively impact its
    performance

Continuum: Pacing Activity

Preference: URGENT

Expressed:
- Considers a few important options before deciding
- Gets things done by taking action quickly and making changes
- Prefers short-term projects requiring quick responses
- Works with a fast-paced, urgent style
- Reacts quickly when frustrated and angered
- Makes most decisions quickly — "Opportunity knocks once"

Strength:
- Taking fast action when opportunities arise that require an immediate decision
- Getting clear quickly on what one believes are key priorities and eliminating options that seem to confuse the issue or delay action

Responses to stress
- May decide things too quickly or impulsively
- May get impatient and short-tempered
- May give up or move on when a little more persistence would have paid off

Preference: STEADY

Expressed:
- Considers many options and alternatives before deciding
- Gets things done by "sticking with them" and persisting
- Prefers long-term projects requiring calculated responses
- Works with an even-paced, consistent style
- Reacts slowly when frustrated and angered
- Makes most decisions cautiously — "Timing is everything"

Strength: • Holding back on decision until better opportunities and deals have time to surface
                                 • Patiently staying open to alternatives and possibilities that show promise and that others may have closed their minds to

Responses to stress • May become anxious when usually calm
                                 • May compromise opinions to avoid conflict
                                 • May hesitate and miss opportunities by waiting too long

Situations to use URGENT approach and to avoid STEADY approach:
   • Group is working on short-term project with tight deadlines
   • Group is expected to find the fastest solutions that work, not necessarily the "best" solutions

Situations to use STEADY approach and to avoid URGENT approach:
   • Group is progressing very well with its work and meeting deadlines
   • Group is expected to find the most effective solutions

Continuum: Dealing with Details

Preference: UNSTRUCTURED

Expressed:
- Tends to postpone organizing and attending to details
- Uses unconventional procedures to accomplish tasks
- Likes plans open and somewhat unpredictable
- Proceeds on projects before reading all the directions
- Takes pride in doing things in new and different ways
- Gets frustrated by too many guidelines and rules

Strength:
- Discovering innovative ways to reach goals that may be outside of the traditional guidelines
- An ability to overlook considerable disorganization and get work done in situations that would bother most people

Responses to stress
- May overlook details and forget to follow up on small tasks
- May look for loopholes in rules and operate independently

Preference: PRECISE

Expressed:
- Tends to organize details in a timely and thorough fashion
- Uses established procedures to accomplish tasks
- Likes plans clearly set and somewhat predictable
- Proceeds on projects only after reading all the directions
- Takes pride in doing things in established, proven ways
- Gets frustrated by ambiguity and lack of specific guidelines

Strength: • The ability to bring order and structure to
                           disorganized situations
                         • Seeing ways to improve systems and policies that
                           help make work flow more evenly and smoothly

Responses to stress • May become overly perfectionistic
                         • Can over worry about small things
                         • May nitpick and get caught up in details

Situations to use UNSTRUCTURED approach and to avoid PRECISE
approach:

- Group operating in very fluid environment with outcomes and
  criteria for success changing frequently
- Group solving problems that have not been studied before, or that
  others have failed to solve

Situations to use PRECISE approach and to avoid UNSTRUCTURED
approach:

- Group operating in very stable environments and precision is
  required
- Group expected to work within a narrow range of possible solutions

Exercise 3.2.1 - Identifying your INSIGHT Inventory® style

In this exercise we want you to identify your preferences as determined by completing the INSIGHT Inventory or by evaluating yourself using the material in the preparation section of this work-out.

In thinking about yourself, do you find that in your work settings you prefer to operate more from an INDIRECT or DIRECT approach? What are examples of your behavior that are consistent with this assessment?

_____

_____

_____

In thinking about yourself, do you find that in your work settings you prefer to operate more from a RESERVED or OUTGOING approach? What are examples of your behavior that are consistent with this assessment?

_____

_____

_____

In thinking about yourself, do you find that in your work settings you prefer to operate more from an URGENT or STEADY approach? What are examples of your behavior that are consistent with this assessment?

_____

_____

_____

In thinking about yourself, do you find that in your work settings you prefer to operate more from an UNSTRUCTURED or PRECISE approach? What are examples of your behavior that are consistent with this assessment?

_____

_____

Exercise 3.2.2 - Your style and your facilitation

Your work-style preferences have a profound effect on your ability to facilitate effectively. Learning to use all eight approaches, depending upon what the group needs, is key to becoming an effective facilitator. In this exercise, we want you to determine how your style affects your ability to facilitate.

Look again at your style preferences. How could using the strengths associated with your preferred style help a group be successful?

_____

_____

_____

How could using the strengths associated with your preferred style get in the way of a group being successful?

_____

_____

_____

How could your tendencies under pressure hinder a group being successful?

_____

_____

_____

What action could you take to reduce the negative effects arising from your tendencies under pressure?

_____

_____

_____

Exercise 3.2.3 - Identifying other styles
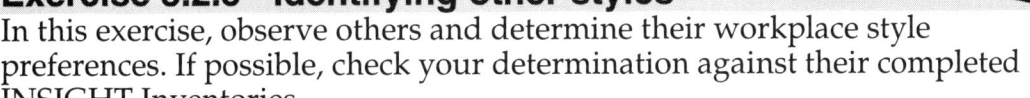

In this exercise, observe others and determine their workplace style preferences. If possible, check your determination against their completed INSIGHT Inventories.

Think about someone with whom you work who operates differently than you. Identify the person's preferences and provide observations to support your conclusion.

_____

_____

_____

At your next meeting with the individual above, make notes about their behaviors. How are these behaviors consistent with your hypothesis about this person's style preferences? How are the behaviors different?

_____

_____

_____

How does this person's behavior help the group operate more effectively? How does it contribute to the group operating less effectively?

_____

_____

_____

How can you operate more effectively with this individual?

_____

_____

_____

Exercise 3.2.4 - Challenges with working with differing styles

In this exercise, identify a problem you have had with another person, especially in a group setting. Use your knowledge of the INSIGHT Inventory style preferences to help you understand why you have had struggles with this person.

Recall a person with whom you have had one or more difficult experiences. How might differences in your work styles have contributed to the difficulties?

_____

_____

_____

Which of the INSIGHT Inventory style preferences of other people have you had the most difficulty with? Why do you think this is the case?

_____

_____

_____

Which of the INSIGHT Inventory style preferences of other people have you found most easy to work with? Why do you think this is the case?

_____

_____

_____

What actions will you take now to work more successfully with people who exhibit style preferences that have troubled you the most?

_____

_____

_____

Exercise 3.2.5 – Facilitating other styles

Different work styles often require different approaches to facilitation. A person who is strongly OUTGOING may struggle with long periods of silence, while a RESERVED person gathers thoughts during a debate. The need to say something will be strong. If the OUTGOING person fills every silence during a discussion, the RESERVED person may not feel any opportunity to contribute. Similar contrasts are experienced with differences on each of the continuums. In this exercise, we want you to think about the challenges of facilitating people with different work-style preferences.

What are some of the challenges in facilitating people who are more INDIRECT? More DIRECT?

What are some of the challenges in facilitating people who are more OUTGOING? More RESERVED?

What are some of the challenges in facilitating people who are more URGENT? More STEADY?

What are some of the challenges in facilitating people who are more UNSTRUCTURED? More PRECISE?

Work-out 3.3 – Challenges with working with differing styles

Preparation

Facilitators continuously monitor how well a group is working together. They help groups gain insight about how individuals' treatment of one another affects their productivity. We know that groups must focus on task in order to be successful. We also know that sustained improvement in productivity only occurs when people treat each other well. Understanding work-style preferences is a key aspect of helping people improve the ways they work together.

Recall the five important facts about work-style preferences:

1. Everyone exhibits preferences for one or more styles.
2. Everyone has the capability to consciously act from a variety of styles.
3. People view the world from their style tendencies.
4. There is no single right or wrong style.
5. Each style has its strengths and weaknesses in particular situations.

Effective facilitators introduce these concepts to groups at appropriate times. Sometimes the situation calls for a training session using the INSIGHT Inventory, one of the DISC instruments, or the Meyers-Briggs Type Inventory (MBTI). Other situations may call for having a brief discussion about one or more of the five points from above. In any case, facilitators take advantage of opportunities to help a group increase its awareness of how its members work together. They help groups experience individual differences as assets that can be used to help everyone.

Exercise 3.3.1 – Exploring the different styles in a group

In this exercise, we want you to think about a group with whom you are familiar. For each person in the group, guess his or her INSIGHT Inventory style preferences. What advantages do each of these individuals bring to the group, in light of their styles? How can the group use these advantages to accomplish its purpose? Think about these questions as you complete the table below. Continue to fill out the table until you have identified three advantages for every group member.

Individual	Style preferences	Advantage to group	How group can use

Exercise 3.3.2 – Challenges with working with differing styles

In this exercise, we want you to facilitate a group discussion about differences in work styles and help people see how their differences can be used as assets instead of liabilities.

What are some ways that the individual style differences of group members have interfered with getting work done in the past?

_____

_____

_____

_____

Which individual style differences of group members seem to have presented the most challenges for the group? Why?

_____

_____

_____

_____

What are some things that you can do, as facilitator, to be more supportive of the individual style differences within your group?

_____

_____

_____

_____

What are some things you will do to capitalize on the group member style differences, rather than to just support or tolerate them?

_____

_____

_____

_____

Cool-down - My self-assessment and action plan

You have completed three work-outs that have helped you know yourself better and improve your ability to help others get their work done. This is one of the most intense units in the entire workbook, forcing you to really "feel the burn" of rigorous exercise. Answer the self-assessment questions below. Then, make an action plan.

For each of the work-outs in this unit, rate your understanding of the subject matter:

Work-out topic	Mastered	Understood	Need more work
3.1 Strengthening your sense of self	A	B	C
3.2 Challenges in understanding differing styles	A	B	C
3.3 Challenges in working with differing styles	A	B	C

What in this unit did you find particularly helpful to improving your ability to effectively use the role of facilitator?

_____

_____

_____

How will you use what you have learned from this unit?

_____

_____

_____

What do you need to learn more about? What steps will you take to do so?

_____

_____

_____

Unit 4
Facilitating Group Development

Warm-up

Effective facilitators recognize which behaviors in groups are normal interactions and which are problems that need to be addressed. They use their presence to help people improve both their productivity and interactions. Facilitators help groups capitalize on conflict rather than be disabled by it.

Effective facilitators also know when to let things take their own course and when to intervene. Striking an appropriate balance is important, and that balance point is different for every group. Some groups respond well to more frequent suggestions while others function more effectively with minimal input from someone using the facilitator role.

In your work as a facilitator, you will find that balance point more easily as you better understand group development. In order to improve your ability to facilitate group development, focus upon the following points in this unit:

4.1 Understand why a group's history is important and learn how to quickly gather information about it.

4.2 Learn practical applications of the 'Orming Model to help a group develop.

4.3 Support a group's development of more collaborative behaviors.

Work-out 4.1 - The importance of group history

Preparation

As a facilitator enters the presence of a group for the first time, he or she must understand the context for this entrance. Even newly formed groups have individuals whose history will affect their functioning. Systematically gathering this information will help a facilitator better understand group behavior and intervene appropriately in the future.

Understanding how a group has dealt with past experiences associated with that process gives powerful insights into helping the group perform better. This history also has a profound effect on the group's ability to work together.

There are a number of questions that a facilitator can ask to find out about a group's history. Even if a facilitator has extensive knowledge of the group, it is wise to confirm the assumptions that accompany this knowledge. The questions do not need to be answered in any particular order. The most interesting part of this process is to see where the responses lead. It is also revealing to see the differences in responses between various group members.

Exercise 4.1.1 - Discovering group history

In this exercise we want you to explore the history of a group and determine how that history may be helping or hindering its performance. Ask several group members the questions below and compare their answers. Feel free to make several copies of this worksheet to complete this exercise.

Group member _____

Why was your group formed? _____

_____

_____

How long ago was your group formed? _____

_____

_____

Has membership in the group changed significantly since it was formed? In the past year? _____

_____

What are examples of successes the group has achieved?

_____

_____

What are examples of failures the group has experienced?

_____

_____

How has leadership emerged within the group? _____

_____

_____

How has the group developed plans to complete its work?

_____

_____

_____

How has conflict been experienced within the group?

_____

_____

_____

How is the group's culture similar and different from the culture of the larger organization? _____

_____

_____

What is the group's Charge? Does everyone agree about the Charge?

_____

_____

_____

Does the group have a Charter?

_____

_____

_____

How will your knowledge of this group's history help you support the group? _____

_____

_____

Work-out 4.2 - The 'Orming Model of group development
Preparation

Groups — whether they are formal teams, work groups, or temporary groups — evolve through four stages: Forming, Storming, Norming, and Performing. By completing the specific tasks for each stage, a group becomes more cohesive and productive. Any time a group experiences changes in membership or leadership, completes a major assignment or gains a new one, it will cycle through the stages again. The figure below illustrates these four stages.

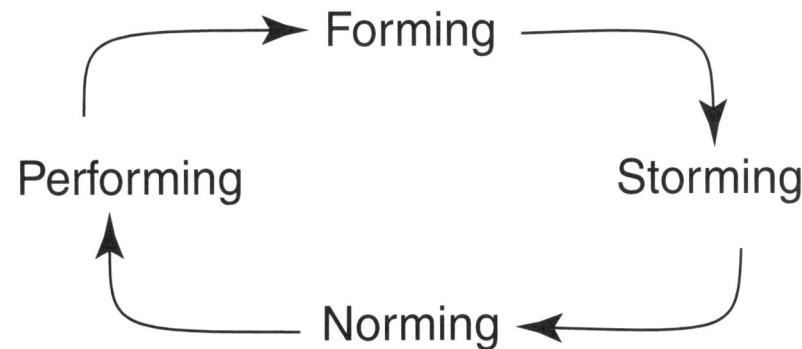

It is essential to determine the current stage of a group and identify what work may have been left undone from previous stages. A primary responsibility of the facilitator is to help the group understand where it is, how it got there, and how it can progress to the next stage. As the group becomes more adept at identifying its stage, it will increase its interpersonal effectiveness, improve its performance, and move through the stages at a more efficient pace.

Forming

Work to be done	• Understand the purpose of the group • Get to know the other group members
Behaviors and dynamics that may be observed	• Uncertainty regarding purpose and goals • Introductions and other socially oriented behavior • Enthusiasm • Tentativeness and testing behavior • Feelings of anxiety • Needing to find a place in the group
Questions to be answered	• Why are we here? • Who are these people?
Problems that will continue to surface if not addressed	• People going in different directions • People not recognizing the people resources within the group

Storming

Work to be done	• Identify what individuals expect from each other and how they expect to work together • State expectations, identify differences and experiences of conflict
Behaviors and dynamics that may be observed	• Conflict within the group • Uncertainty regarding roles • Overzealous behavior • Strong resistance to group formation • Frustration • Competition between individuals in the group and formation of cliques
Questions to be answered	• What do I expect from others? • What do they expect from me?
Problems that will continue to surface if not addressed	• People getting upset because their expectations are not being met • People feeling they have to do too much of the work • People feeling they are not an important or useful part of the group

Norming

Work to be done	• Resolve differences in what members expect of each other and how they will work together • Establish ground rules, prepare a group charter, define how the group will work together
Behaviors and dynamics that may be observed	• Negotiation • Development of a commonly held purpose • Group spirit begins to form as the group begins to work together • Members are supportive of each other • The group sets and accomplishes goals • Harmony, trust, and respect are developing
Questions to be answered	• How are we going to work together?
Problems that will continue to surface if not addressed	• Group does not have agreement about how it will work together • Group members working at cross-purposes with other group members

Performing

Work to be done	• Tasks that will lead the group to accomplishing its Charge and Charter • Continued attention on how the group is working together
Behaviors and dynamics that may be observed	• Clear role definition and ability to "flex" between roles • Collaboration • Interdependence • Feeling group strength • Consistent, excellent performance • High group member satisfaction
Questions to be answered	• How will we know when we have been successful?
Problems that will continue to surface if not addressed	• Work not getting done on time and/or at an acceptable quality • Group unable to recognize or celebrate its accomplishments

Exercise 4.2.1 - Identifying a group's stage

The 'Orming Model provides facilitators with a powerful way to understand the behaviors and dynamics they observe in groups. In this exercise we want you to observe a group and determine which stage of the 'Orming model it is in.

What stage is the group in? _____

_____

_____

_____

What do you observe that leads to this conclusion? _____

_____

_____

_____

_____

What work, if any, from previous stages needs to be completed?

_____

_____

_____

_____

What can you do to help the group complete the work associated with this and previous stages? _____

_____

_____

_____

Work-out 4.3 - Supporting development of more collaborative behaviors

Preparation

By observing groups, facilitators are able to discern their prevalent patterns of behaviors. **Effective facilitators observe at two levels. At the first level, facilitators simply watch particular exchanges among group members**. They are then available and prepared to help the exchange if it becomes unproductive. This level of observation requires the full presence and attention of the facilitator at that moment. Some exchanges can be so riveting that facilitators forget to intervene when they should. Not getting caught up in the drama of these exchanges is a skill that effective facilitators cultivate.

At the **second level, facilitators must accumulate their first-level observations over time and then interpret them**. This requires reflection to detect patterns in the ways group members interact. Was a particular outburst from one group member an isolated incident or was it part of a pattern? What about the way the group worked easily to consensus when solving the latest problem? Why are several group members not talking to each other during group meetings?

The effective facilitator selectively shares these first- and second-level observations with the group in a process known as *reflection*. Using reflection appropriately is one of the most artistic aspects of facilitation. Different groups and different circumstances require different types of reflection. When reflecting observations to the group, the facilitator should begin by saying something like, "What I just heard was" or "This is what I just saw happen." By using reflection, the facilitator helps the group pay attention to the way it works together. The group may not agree with the facilitator's observations or interpretations. The effective facilitator reflects in ways that allow the group members to respond and draw their own conclusions. Reflection is one of the strongest ways a facilitator can model helpful behavior.

One of the patterns a facilitator will observe is the common ways group members relate to each other. These relationship patterns may range from adversarial to partnering. We have found it helpful to categorize these patterns to help facilitators both better understand their groups and decide what action they can take to help the groups be more productive. **The figure below presents these categories on the adversarial-to-partnering continuum**. Any of these forms of interaction can and will occur at times in every group. This is normal and natural.

What is important is which type of relationship is most common. Groups that demonstrate the more adversarial interactions are less able to work together effectively. They are likely to become stuck as a chance grouping or false group. They will find it harder to build the interdependence that characterizes the groups who progress to fully functioning groups. They tend to look at specific solutions in terms of who succeeds and who fails: a win-lose scenario.

The more partnering behavior on the right side of the figure is typical of groups that are advancing in their development or maintenance as fully functioning groups. They value partnering and are looking for solutions where *everyone* can be successful: a win-win scenario.

6 C Model Relationship Model

Adversarial	Coercion	Confrontation	Coexistence	Cooperation	Collaboration	Co-Ownership	Partnering

Win - Lose   Win - Win

Coercion	The use of power to force a desired outcome.
Confrontation	Open disagreement.
Coexistence	People agree not to cross into each other's territory.
Cooperation	A focus on individual tasks, with some assistance between people.
Collaboration	Pulling together for the common good. Finding solutions together.
Co-Ownership	All group members feel 100% responsible for the group's success.

The challenge for every facilitator is to help groups progress to the point where they exhibit the types of relationships appropriate for the type of group they seek to be. Groups aspiring to reach fully functioning status need to exhibit collaborative and co-ownership behavior.

Exercise 4.3.1 - Determining the level of collaboration within a group

In this exercise we want you to help a group evaluate its position on the 6-C model and make a plan for moving towards more partnering relationships. Start by drawing the 6-C model on a flip-chart and explaining what it represents. Then, facilitate a discussion around the questions below. If you do not have a group with whom you can have this discussion, answer the questions based upon your observations of a work group with whom you are familiar.

Ask each individual to choose the position on the 6-C model that she or he feels best represents the group. Have them do this silently, on their own.

_____

_____

Mark the answers on the flip-chart. Ask the group to interpret the results. Record your observations of the discussion below, after the group convenes this meeting. _____

_____

_____

Ask the group if they wish to move to the right on the model. If their answer is "yes," then ask them to identify the steps they will take.

_____

_____

_____

After the group convenes, describe below what it was like to facilitate this discussion. What would you do differently next time?

_____

_____

_____

_____

Exercise 4.3.2 - The "TARGET" approach to group development

The challenge for every facilitator is to help groups and teams progress to the point where they exhibit the types of relationships appropriate for the type of group that they are seeking to be. To promote this progress, it is helpful to know what contributes to working in a more partnering approach.

Trust is one of the most important characteristics of collaborative groups. A practical way for facilitators to help groups develop trust and to act more consistently on the partnering side of the continuum is to use the Target Approach to Group Development, as illustrated in the figure below.

Truth

Accountability

Respect

Growth

Empowerment

Trust

Successfully building on each of the first five areas depicted in the TARGET model leads to trust within a group. Members of fully functioning groups trust each other. They know they can count on each other. Facilitators must be concerned with the level of trust in their groups. Although trust appears to be very intangible and often fragile, facilitators can help people build their trust in one another. One of the most helpful steps is helping groups identify where strong trust already exists and where trust is weakest. These are often difficult discussions that require close attention by facilitators to keep them productive.

In this exercise, we want you to help a group assess one or more of the elements of the TARGET Model, using the TARGET Model Worksheet on the next page.

TARGET Model Worksheet

Review the TARGET Model. Facilitate a discussion with the group that helps it develop a common definition of each element of the TARGET Model.

Ask the group to choose one element from the TARGET Model that it will evaluate.

Record here the element to be evaluated: _____

Ask each individual in the group to rate, on a scale of 1 to 7, this element of the TARGET Model relative to the way people currently work together. Give them an opportunity to make their rating alone, in silence. If they are using this worksheet, they can use the scale below.

1	2	3	4	5	6	7
No trust			Moderate trust			Total trust

Next, gather each individual's response anonymously. Record the range of responses on a flip-chart, using the scale above.

Ask the group to interpret the results. _____

_____

_____

_____

Once the group has interpreted the results of its informal survey, ask it to determine specific actions it will take to strengthen this TARGET element within the group. _____

_____

_____

_____

Cool-down - My self-assessment and action plan

You have completed three work-outs that will help you support the development of groups you facilitate. Answer the self-assessment questions below. Then, make an action plan to both apply your learning and improve your mastery of the subject matter of this unit.

For each of the work-outs in this unit, rate your understanding of the subject matter:

Work-out topic	Mastered	Understood	Need more work
4.1 Understanding and using group history	A	B	C
4.2 'Orming Model	A	B	C
4.3 6-C Model and TARGET Model	A	B	C

What in this unit did you find particularly helpful to improving your ability to effectively use the role of facilitator?

_____

_____

_____

How will you use what you have learned from this unit?

_____

_____

_____

What do you need to learn more about? What steps will you take to do so?

_____

_____

_____

Unit 5
Dealing with Conflict

Warm-up

Every group experiences conflict. The challenge is handling it effectively. Conflict is most often identified when there is a verbal and/or possibly physically violent clash between individuals or groups. Some people find these dramatic clashes to be exciting, while others seek to avoid them. People tend to take these types of conflict very personally. Facilitators need to be aware that conflict occurs in groups in many more forms than open, highly emotional clashes between people.

Groups struggle with conflict. They assume that conflict is inherently bad and harmony is required for group success. If this were true, then any open expression of conflict would be a sign of a poorly performing group. This is not true! It is not the open expression of conflict that is the sign of a poorly performing group, it is not using those differences effectively that drags down their performance. For this reason, a facilitator does a group a disservice by pushing a group through a conflict too quickly or avoiding it altogether.

Conflict is often associated with fighting, battles, even wars. At the most civil level it is associated with people being incompatible. Our approach to conflict is in stark contrast to this traditional definition. We define conflict as **situations where two or more people appear to have different desires, needs, wants, opinions, or beliefs**.

Thus, **conflict is a normal process that occurs many times every day in the life of a group**. People deal with their differences successfully all the time. The more they can recognize their ability to handle conflict at this level, the more confidence they can have in dealing with its more dramatic forms.

Effective facilitators help people capitalize on their conflicts. Using conflict in this way makes it a valuable resource rather than personal battles in which there are winners and losers. Having winners and losers forces people apart, making them less interdependent.

In order to improve your ability to help groups have positive experiences with conflict, focus on the following points in this unit:

5.1 Reflect on your experiences and observations of conflict.
5.2 Understand the use of different conflict response modes.
5.3 Help a group resolve a conflict using the conflict resolution process.

Work-out 5.1 - Your experiences and observations of conflict
Preparation

There are people who find conflict to be exciting, something that invigorates them. Conflict may be better than "another boring meeting." Some may simply like to create situations where they can "win." For others, conflict is a sign that someone cares about what is happening. Still others are greatly distressed at the slightest difference of opinion.

Conflict has as many faces as those who experience it. However people experience it, conflict is a necessary part of the life of healthy groups and organizations. Ask yourself, "What would things be like if no one ever disagreed?" Would your group and organization do its best work if everyone agreed with the first idea, the first plan? Of course not!

Synergy — the whole is greater than the sum of the parts — is created in organizations where people build on the ideas and work of others. The differences stimulate people to new levels of creativity, which then stimulates someone else to take it further.

It is in not dealing with it effectively that conflict becomes the dreaded event that must be avoided. The challenge is to respond to conflict in ways that help groups and organizations benefit from their differences rather than becoming disabled by them. Meeting this challenge greatly enhances a group's interdependence.

One very important job of the facilitator is to help the group understand that conflict and its successful resolution is a requirement for groups to produce more than simply the sum of their individual efforts. The facilitator needs to not fear conflict. He or she must understand how others approach conflict and be prepared to introduce tools and processes that help them work through conflict to a positive result where everybody wins.

Exercise 5.1.1 - Your personal experiences with conflict

Your experiences with conflict affect your ability to deal with it. In this exercise we want you to recall your personal experiences with conflict.

When you think about conflict, what personal experiences immediately come to mind? _____

_____

_____

_____

What feelings do you experience as you recall these personal experiences?

_____

_____

_____

_____

What was the worst outcome you ever experienced from a conflict situation at work? _____

_____

_____

_____

Describe the best outcome from a conflict situation you have ever experienced at work. _____

_____

_____

_____

Exercise 5.1.2 - Conflict in group settings

In this exercise we want you to recall and/or observe conflict in a group setting.

Describe a current conflict that you have observed within a group at work.

_____

_____

_____

_____

How do you know it is a conflict? What is occurring to convince you that a conflict exists? _____

_____

_____

_____

How would the group improve its productivity by resolving the conflict?

_____

_____

_____

_____

How would the group improve its interdependence by resolving the conflict? _____

_____

_____

_____

_____

Work-out 5.2 - Thomas-Kilmann conflict response modes

Preparation

Conflict situations can be challenging. Even relatively minor conflicts can be tough to work through if the people involved refuse to consider other options. Fortunately, there is a model that helps us understand the range of normal behaviors we can expect to encounter.

Kenneth Thomas and Ralph Kilmann examined the fundamental ways people approach conflict. They found that people prefer specific ways of dealing with conflict. In these situations, Thomas and Kilmann described a person's behavior along two basic dimensions: (1) *assertiveness*, the extent to which the individual attempts to satisfy his or her own concerns, and (2) *cooperativeness*, the extent to which the individual attempts to satisfy the other person's concerns. These two basic dimensions of behavior can be used to define five specific methods of dealing with conflicts. These five "conflict handling modes" are shown below.

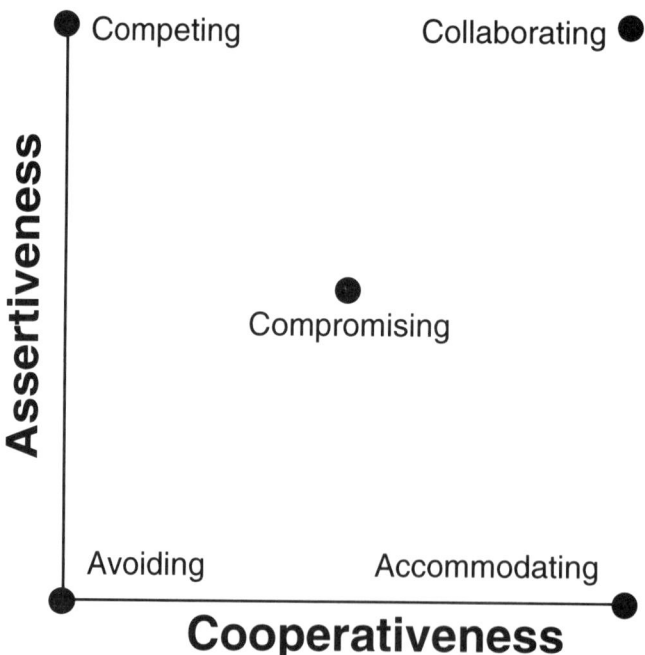

Avoiding **is unassertive and uncooperative.** The individual does not immediately pursue his or her own concerns or those of the other person. He or she does not address conflict. Avoiding might take the form of diplomatically sidestepping an issue, postponing an issue until a better time, or simply withdrawing from a threatening situation.

Competing **is assertive and uncooperative.** An individual pursues his or her own concerns at the expense of others'. This is a power-oriented mode in which one uses whatever power seems appropriate to win one's own position: ability to argue; rank; economic sanctions. Competing might mean standing up for your rights, defending a position which you believe is correct, or simply trying to win.

Accommodating **is unassertive and cooperative.** When accommodating, an individual neglects his or her own concerns to satisfy the concerns of the other person; there is an element of self-sacrifice in this mode. Accommodating might take the form of selfless generosity; obeying another person's order when one would prefer not to; or yielding to another's point of view.

Collaborating **is both assertive and cooperative.** Collaborating involves an attempt to work with the other person to find some solution that fully satisfies the concerns of both persons. It means digging into an issue to identify the underlying concerns of the two individuals and to find an alternative that meets both sets of concerns. Collaborating between two persons might take the form of exploring a disagreement to learn from each other's insights, committing to resolve some condition which would otherwise have them competing for resources, or confronting and trying to find a creative solution to an interpersonal problem.

Compromising **is intermediate in both assertiveness and cooperativeness.** The objective is to find some quick, mutually acceptable solution that partially satisfies both parties. It falls on a middle ground between competing and accommodating. Compromising gives up more than competing but less than accommodating. It addresses an issue more directly than avoiding, but does not explore it in as much depth as collaborating. Compromising might mean splitting the difference, exchanging concessions, or seeking a quick middle-ground position.

Each of us is capable of all five conflict-handling modes; none of us can be characterized as having a single, rigid style of dealing with conflict. However, every individual is more comfortable and effective with some modes more than others. This preference is often related to a person's temperament and experience. The conflict-handling behaviors that an individual uses are therefore a result of both his or her personal predispositions and the requirements of specific situations.

Each of the five modes are the best choice in different situations. The challenge is to choose and use the best one for a particular situation. This can be especially difficult when we have a very strong preference for one of the modes. The exercises that follow help you identify the circumstances in which one mode will be your best choice.

Exercise 5.2.1 - Using the competing mode

In this exercise we want you to explore use of the competing mode in a conflict situation. **In this mode, people focus on their perspective, regardless of others**. It can be used effectively in the following situations:

- When quick, decisive action is vital (e.g., emergencies)
- On important issues where unpopular courses of action need implementation (e.g., supporting unpopular rules, insisting on a particular course of action)
- On issues vital to team welfare when you know you are right
- To protect yourself against people who take advantage of noncompetitive behavior

Describe a situation at work where using this mode would be appropriate. Be sure to describe the outcome you want. _____

_____

_____

How could using this mode help you achieve the outcome you desire?

_____

_____

_____

What might you do or say as a facilitator in the above situation to help the group appropriately use this conflict response mode?

_____

_____

_____

Exercise 5.2.2 - Using the compromising mode

In this exercise we want you to explore use of the compromising mode in a conflict situation. **In this mode, everyone gives a little**. It can be used effectively in the following situations:

* When goals are moderately important, but not worth the effort or potential disruption of more assertive modes
* When two opponents with equal power are strongly committed to perceived mutually exclusive goals (e.g., labor–management bargaining)
* To achieve temporary settlements to complex issues
* To arrive at quick solutions under time pressures

Describe a situation at work where using this mode would be appropriate. Be sure to describe the outcome you want. _____

_____

_____

How could using this mode help you achieve the outcome you desire?

_____

_____

_____

What might you do or say as a facilitator in the above situation to help the group appropriately use this conflict response mode?

_____

_____

_____

Exercise 5.2.3 - Using the collaborating mode

In this exercise we want you to explore use of the collaborating mode in a conflict situation. **In this mode, everyone works to get what they want, and sometimes end up with even more.** It can be used effectively in the following situations:

- To find an integrative solution when both sets of concerns are too important to be compromised
- When your objective is to learn, test your assumptions, and understand others
- To blend insights from people with different perspectives on a problem
- To gain commitment by incorporating others' concerns into a consensus decision
- To work through feelings that have been interfering with a personal relationship

Describe a situation at work where using this mode would be appropriate. Be sure to describe the outcome you want. _____

_____

_____

How could using this mode help you achieve the outcome you desire?

_____

_____

_____

What might you do or say as a facilitator in the above situation to help the group appropriately use this conflict response mode?

_____

_____

_____

Exercise 5.2.4 - Using the avoiding mode

In this exercise we want you to explore use of the avoiding mode in a conflict situation. **In this mode, you do not address the situation at the present time.** It can be used effectively in the following situations:

*   When an issue is not important or when other more important issues are pressing
*   When you perceive no chance of satisfying your concerns
*   When the potential damage of confronting a conflict outweighs the benefits of its resolution
*   To let people cool down, to reduce tensions to a productive level, and to regain perspective and composure
*   When others can resolve the conflict without you

Describe a situation at work where using this mode would be appropriate. Be sure to describe the outcome you want. _____

_____

_____

How could using this mode help you achieve the outcome you desire?

_____

_____

_____

What might you do or say as a facilitator in the above situation to help the group appropriately use this conflict response mode?

_____

_____

_____

Exercise 5.2.5 - Using the accommodating mode

In this exercise we want you to explore use of the accommodating mode in a conflict situation. **In this mode, you focus on others' perspectives, regardless of your own.** It can be used effectively in the following situations:

- When you realize that you are wrong, to allow a better position to be heard, to learn from others, and to show that you are reasonable
- When the issue is much more important to the other person than to yourself, to satisfy the needs of others, and as a goodwill gesture
- To build up social credits for later issues that are more important to you
- To aid in the development of team members by allowing them to experiment and learn from their own mistakes

Describe a situation at work where using this mode would be appropriate. Be sure to describe the outcome you want. _____

_____

_____

_____

How could using this mode help you achieve the outcome you desire?

_____

_____

_____

What might you do or say as a facilitator in the above situation to help the group appropriately use this conflict response mode?

_____

_____

_____

Work-out 5.3 - Conflict resolution process

Preparation

Resolving conflict is essential to helping people reach closure around important projects or events. As we discussed in Unit 2, helping people achieve closure is fundamental to helping them be productive group members. Without this, unresolved differences can build up over time and minor events can create major explosions.

Resolving conflict means that the issue is considered closed by the people concerned about it. Resolution is demonstrated by people not engaging in the conflict (avoidance), agreeing to the other person's solution (accommodation), gaining his or her own solution (competing), agreeing to a middle ground (compromise), or creating a win-win solution (collaboration). Achieving a compromise or collaboration solution does not happen by "magic." It happens because people care enough and know how to work through a process. The five steps to the conflict resolution process are summarized below.

Step 1. Expression of differences

- Statements and/or questions between two or more people
- Thoughts in the minds of one or more group members
- Feelings that something is unexpected or undesired

Step 2. Awareness of conflict

- Causes each person to initiate one of the five conflict modes
- If Avoiding or Accommodating is chosen, the individual does not pursue the conflict further.
- If Competing is chosen, this individual tries to jump two steps and impose a resolution.
- If Compromising or Collaborating is chosen, then the individuals will move to the next step in the conflict resolution process.

Step 3. Clarification of differences

- Which conflict mode is used has a big impact on this step
- Those using the Compromising mode seek information to determine the most successful bargaining strategy.
- Those using Collaborating seek to understand the essence of the outcome that the other wants.

- In this step, individuals seek to clarify where the true differences exist. They ask questions of one another in an effort to truly understand the other, and make clear their own position. The key here is to give all parties a chance to be heard. The difference between "clarification of differences" and a shouting match is that, in this step, people are listening to one another intently.

Step 4. Agreement on commonality
- Points of agreement are openly discussed
- Provides reasons for continuing the work of finding a resolution
- People will pursue Collaborative or Compromise resolutions of conflicts when they experience building on some form of existing agreement. Whether it is "By resolving this conflict well, we can create an even better solution" or "We have to resolve this or we can't finish this project," this agreement is necessary.
- Often, when there is a disagreement, people jump to the conclusion that they disagree about everything or nearly everything about the subject. Usually, they agree upon more than they realize. This step makes it possible to discover just how much, or little, people agree.
- To get to the resolution, the conflict resolution process requires both parties to present their positions as clearly as possible and listen to other's positions.

Step 5. Resolution of conflict
- If you go through Steps 1–4, this happens pretty easily.
- Commit to choose a resolution — and then stick with it.
- Agree to come to closure on the conflict and complete the work at hand.

Practical, helpful questions to ask to work through the process
1. What is the issue or problem?
   (How the issue or problem is stated often determines the outcome.)
2. Where do we not agree?
   (Areas of disagreement must be identified so that they can be dealt with as separate issues or problems to be resolved.)
3. Where (as we discuss the issue) can we agree?
   (Areas of agreement are identified as a way of establishing a good foundation for the eventual solution.)

4. Can we develop options that take advantage of the areas where we agree, and bring us closer in the areas where we disagree?
    (Options are developed to take advantage of the areas of disagreement.)
5. What action(s) will we take as next steps that will resolve the conflict?
    (Actions represent what each party will do as a result of the discussion: What by Whom by When.)

A word about compromise

Compromise is often positioned as the best possible outcome of a conflict situation. As we have seen, it is simply one of five good ways to resolve a conflict, depending upon the situation.

Going for compromise means negotiating. Negotiating is built on the premise that "I want to trade away the things that mean less to me to maintain the things that mean more to me." Therefore, negotiating requires withholding information about what is most important because that knowledge can be used against me. It is because of this dynamic that negotiation rarely reaches even an optimal compromise since all the key information and options never get out on the table. Negotiations usually stop whenever the first acceptable solution is discovered. There is no reason to pursue the process to find a better solution.

There are times when compromise is the best mode to choose. The negotiations that follow often lead to an acceptable outcome in a relatively short time. Facilitators should be aware of the strengths and weaknesses of this mode. The series of actions and questions in the table below will help you support conflict resolution.

Practical things you can do to help a group work through the conflict resolution process

Steps	Facilitator action	Facilitator questions
Expression of Differences	Observe the verbal and nonverbal communication in the group.	What expressions of differences do you observe?
Awareness of Conflict	Identify the conflict situation to the group and give the group an opportunity to use the rest of the conflict resolution steps.	What is the issue or problem? How the issue or problem is stated often determines the outcome.
Clarification of Differences	Help the group gather information about either the bargaining points or the essences of what it needs for a win-win solution.	Where do we not agree? Areas of disagreement must be identified so they can be dealt with as separate issues or problems to be resolved.
Agreement on Commonality	Assist the group to identify points at which it is in agreement.	Where can we agree? Areas of agreement are identified as a way of establishing a good foundation for the eventual solution.
Resolution of Conflict	Keep the discussion focused on reaching agreement and help the group recognize when it has achieved agreement.	Can we develop options that take advantage of the areas where we agree, and bring us closer in the areas where we disagree? Options are developed to take advantage of where there had been disagreement. What will each party do as a result of the discussion: What by Whom by When.

Exercise 5.3.1 - Observing a conflict

In this exercise we want you to observe a group in conflict and evaluate what is happening using the framework of the conflict resolution process.

Identify a conflict situation in a group. What did you observe?

_____

_____

What was being said? What words were being used? _____

_____

_____

What was the tone of the voices? Were voices raised? Lowered?

_____

_____

What were the nonverbal signals? (body posture, facial expressions, etc.)

_____

_____

How far in the conflict resolution process did the group get? What helped or hindered it? _____

_____

_____

What should the group do to resolve the conflict? _____

_____

_____

Exercise 5.3.2 - Working through the conflict resolution process

In this exercise we want you to help a group work through the conflict resolution process.

Describe a conflict situation for a group you work with. Note the expression of differences that first called the conflict to your attention.

_____

_____

_____

Help the group become aware of the conflict by calling attention to it. Invite the group to participate in a process to resolve it. How did taking this step differ from past attempts to work through conflict within the group?

_____

_____

_____

Help the group clarify its differences. What about this step was hard for you and/or the group? How did clarifying differences help? _____

_____

_____

_____

Help group members come to agreement about what they hold in common about this subject. Was there agreement on the actual topic that was in conflict? What was held in agreement at that time? _____

_____

_____

_____

If the group finds no agreement on the specific subject matter, then it may have to look above or beyond that subject to find the things it has in agreement. If you did this, what things did the group find in common at this level? _____

_____

_____

Given the subject of the conflict, and the things that group members have in common, help the group propose some potential resolutions to the conflict. Record those potential solutions below. _____

_____

_____

_____

Help the group identify the best resolution, or create a new resolution from the collection of possibilities. At this point, the group is close to finding a resolution, if it has thoroughly completed the first four steps in the process. Record your observations of its conversations at this point in the process.

_____

_____

_____

Record below the resolution of this conflict. _____

_____

_____

_____

In what ways could you improve the way you used the process?

_____

_____

_____

Cool-down - My self-assessment and action plan

You have completed three work-outs that will enable you to support the use of conflict as an important tool for creating group development. Answer the self-assessment questions below. Then, make an action plan to both apply your learning and improve your mastery of the subject matter of this unit.

For each of the work-outs in this unit, rate your understanding of the subject matter:

Work-out topic	Mastered	Understood	Need more work
5.1 Interpreting your experiences with conflict	A	B	C
5.2 Conflict response modes	A	B	C
5.3 Conflict resolution process	A	B	C

What in this unit did you find particularly helpful to improving your ability to effectively use the role of facilitator?

_____

_____

_____

How will you use what you have learned from this unit?

_____

_____

_____

What do you need to learn more about? What steps will you take to do so?

_____

_____

Unit 6
Process: Planning, Solving Problems, Making Decisions, Finishing Work

Warm-up

Process is the fourth element of the facilitation model. We define process as **what a facilitator does to help a group get its work done**. This process-oriented work, such as planning, solving problems, making decisions, and finishing work, has traditionally been the primary focus of publications and training classes on facilitation. While facilitators certainly must demonstrate expertise with these tools, they also must simultaneously use the other elements of the facilitation model. For example, a project team responsible for developing a new fan blade for a jet engine will want to use a highly detailed approach to planning its project. A work group at a nonprofit organization, where individuals "wear several hats," will likely respond better to a simpler, faster planning process. The facilitator must know the task the group needs to complete, be prepared to respond to different work styles, and understand the group. By doing so, the facilitator will use the best process tool for the situation.

There are a variety of excellent publications that describe in detail specific facilitation tools such as brainstorming, consensus, and process mapping. We will not review those particular tools in detail here. Instead, we will focus on the fundamental facilitation processes. Regardless of the complexity of a group's task, facilitators must understand how to apply these processes. This is where the art and science of facilitation come together. In this unit, you will learn about helping groups:

6.1 Plan projects.
6.2 Solve problems and make decisions.
6.3 Finish work.
6.4 Plan effective meetings.

Work-out 6.1 - Helping a group draft a plan

Preparation

We see so many groups rush forward with their work, failing to plan ahead. This wastes time and money later on. The frantic pace of work these days is a real barrier to effective planning. And yet, with the pressure on to increase revenues and profits, organizations cannot afford the costs of poor planning.

This is where an effective facilitator is invaluable to a group. **Groups need to quickly make plans and follow them in order to successfully complete their tasks.** Effective facilitators help groups make their planning a good investment. They provide a framework to help groups plan efficiently. Facilitators push groups to be rigorous so their plans produce the results they want. To help groups plan effectively, facilitators ask the following questions:

1. **What are you trying to accomplish? What is the goal of the project?**
2. **When does the project need to be completed?**
3. **What tasks need to be completed in order to achieve the goal? Who should be accountable for the completion of each task? When does each task need to be finished in order to keep the project on track?**
4. **How will we know when we have accomplished the goal? What will it look like when the goal is successfully completed?**

The Charter, consisting of a group's purpose, goals, roles, and procedures, is really a large-scale plan. It helps a group be clear about its overall purpose, the goals it will accomplish, roles that help people work together, and procedures it will use to get things done. A group that has completed a Charter can build upon that experience to plan projects. Keep in mind the principles you learned in Unit 2 of this workbook as you facilitate other planning activities.

Exercise 6.1.1 - Evaluating a project plan

"If you don't have time to do it right, you sure don't have time to do it over!" said the wise project engineer. Effective facilitators help their groups avoid the rework that is caused by poor planning. By using a systematic approach, facilitators help groups improve their plans and avoid costly mistakes. In this exercise we want you to evaluate a project plan on which you or a colleague is currently working.

What is the goal of the project? _____

_____

Is there a commonly held understanding of the goal within the group?

_____

Are the tasks clearly defined? _____

_____

Is there an individual responsible for every task? _____

_____

Does every task have a deadline? _____

_____

Is every task necessary in order for the project goal to be accomplished?

_____

Is the collection of tasks sufficient to accomplish the project goal?

_____

Is there a written description of what it will look like when the project is successful? _____

What recommendations do you have for improving this project plan?

_____

_____

Exercise 6.1.2 - Helping a group create a project plan

Projects vary greatly due to differences in their complexity, size, and variance. Every project, regardless of these characteristics, needs a set of tasks organized into a schedule, people and other resources assigned to it, and a budget. Typically, a facilitator is called upon to help a group define a project's overall goal, identify the main tasks that will be required to accomplish the goal, and formulate a basic schedule. The further details of resource assignment and budget are usually handled by project management professionals, although facilitators can certainly help with these aspects of project planning as well.

In this exercise we ask you to help a group create the basic elements of a project plan: the project goal, the primary tasks, and a basic schedule.

What is the goal of the project? _____

_____

_____

What are the tasks to be completed in order to accomplish the goal?
(Hint: First, have the group brainstorm the task list. Then, have them organize the list.)

When should each task be completed? _____

How long will each task take to complete? Have we given sufficient time to complete each task? _____

Who should be responsible for each task? _____

_____

_____

What is a logical sequence in which to organize these tasks? _____

What will it look like when the project goal is accomplished? What difference will it make? _____

_____

Work-out 6.2 - Helping people solve problems and make decisions

Preparation

Solving problems and making decisions are everyday occurrences for groups. Groups who have moved up the group development curve have rigorous, efficient methods for problem solving and decision making. Groups that are further down the curve tend to struggle with solving problems and making decisions. A group that uses effective procedures for problem solving and decision making will be more productive and more highly interdependent.

Effective facilitators help by providing a systematic approach to solving problems and making decisions. The following approach helps groups solve their problems by answering a logical sequence of questions:

1. **What is the problem? Accurately describe the problem itself.**
2. **How bad is it? Gather information — both qualitative and quantitative data.**
3. **What do we think is causing the problem? Determine the most important factors contributing to the problem.**
4. **What would it look like if we did not have this problem? Describe what would be happening if things were going well.**
5. **How can we solve this problem? Create action steps to solve the problem.**

One of the biggest challenges groups face is the pressure to produce instant solutions. What can a facilitator do to help groups cope with this pressure and solve problems successfully? Helping a group work on the right problem first, rather than focusing on a symptom of the problem, will save time. Therefore, position the problem-solving process as a time-saver.

Using the right combination of tools (for example, brainstorming, multivoting, cause-effect diagram), facilitators can help groups work through the first four steps of the problem-solving process in as little as 30 minutes. With practice, groups learn to solve problems more quickly and increase the odds that the solutions will be successful.

In the course of planning projects and solving problems groups make hundreds of decisions. Some are minor, the responsibility of only one group member. Others are major, requiring commitment from people outside of the group. Below is a simple four-step process facilitators use to help groups make decisions.

1. **Define what is to be decided.**
2. **Choose who will make the decision.**
3. **Determine the criteria against which the decision will be made.**
4. **Make the decision and follow through with it.**

Be clear about what decision is to be made, and then choose who will make it. Some decisions are best made by individuals, while other decisions require using a consensus process with all group members. Regardless of who makes the decision, a group must agree to stand behind it.

Criteria are used to guide decision making. When the criteria are clear, it is more likely that a decision will produce the desired outcome. Individuals will apply their own criteria to every decision they make, whether or not they are aware of it. Groups get stuck in their decision-making process very often because they fail to agree on criteria, or set them at all. For example, criteria could include staying within the project budget, being done with the task on time, or staying within specification.

The fourth step in the decision-making process, make the decision and follow through with it, is the point at which the decision-making process sometimes goes off track. People are so relieved to have reached a decision that they forget to assign someone the responsibility of carrying it out! **Making a decision is akin to taking on a new task.** When a decision is actually made, it usually requires one or more people to follow through and take some action. Thus, someone has to be responsible for completing the tasks that come from a decision. Facilitators help groups by suggesting that someone take responsibility for following through on a decision.

Exercise 6.2.1 - Helping a group solve a problem

In this exercise we want you to help a group solve a problem. We suggest that you start with something that is manageable and not too difficult. Use the series of questions below as you facilitate the discussion.

Describe the problem. _____

_____

_____

What is happening now? (Hint: you may need to facilitate a very structured discussion, literally having people take turns, if the situation is emotionally charged.)

What measures or other information do we have that tell us about what is happening now?

What is contributing to the problem? (Hint: a cause-effect analysis, or fishbone diagram, is a useful tool for this situation.)

What would be happening if this problem were solved? (Hint: this discussion should lead to the group setting a goal.)

What specific actions do we need to take to solve this problem? (Hint: this discussion should lead to creating a list of tasks to accomplish the goal.)

After this discussion, make some notes below about your performance as a facilitator. What did you do well? What would you do differently?

_____

_____

_____

_____

_____

_____

Exercise 6.2.2 – Your personal decision-making process

Understanding your personal decision-making process will help you facilitate the process with others. In this exercise we want you to consciously use the decision-making process to decide something for yourself.

Make a list of decisions you must make in the near future.

_____

_____

Choose one of the above decisions, and list the criteria you will use to make it. _____

_____

Who is affected by your decision? _____

_____

_____

What could happen if your decision does not produce the result you want?

_____

_____

How will you respond to others if they disagree with your decision?

_____

_____

When must your decision be made? _____

_____

_____

What is your decision at this time? _____

_____

_____

Exercise 6.2.3 - Helping a group make a decision

Perhaps the most important decision any group makes involves hiring. A good decision brings a new person who can make important contributions to the group. A bad decision is counterproductive for both the new hire and the group. While not all decisions are as critical as this, it is still important for groups to develop an efficient decision-making process. In this exercise we want you to help a group make a decision. Use the series of questions below to help them work through the process.

What is the group going to decide?

What criteria will you use to make your decision?

Who is affected by your decision, both inside of and outside of the group?

What could happen if your decision does not produce the result you want?

How will you respond to others if they disagree with your decision?

When must your decision be carried out?

What is your decision at this time?

Does your decision fit the criteria you established?

Work-out 6.3 - Finishing work — Achieving closure

Preparation

The ultimate objective of planning, solving problems, and making decisions is to finish work. Finishing work, literally completing it and declaring it to be done, is fundamental to the success of every individual, group, and organization. **Helping a group finish its work, sometimes referred to as reaching or achieving closure, is one of the most important things facilitators do**. We discussed closure at length in Unit 2, when we were focusing on clarifying and completing tasks. We revisit closure again in this unit because finishing work is a fundamental process that facilitators must understand.

With so much work to do, **groups often forget to acknowledge what they have accomplished**. As soon as one task is complete, another takes its place. Busy groups can get so caught up in setting and achieving goals that they forget to step back, even for a moment, and look at what they have accomplished. This can drain the energy from a group, leading to a loss in productivity.

What does "finishing work" look like? Fulfilling the purpose of a meeting, completing an action step, finalizing a plan, solving a problem, or making a decision are all examples of finishing work. Completing goals from the Charter and ultimately fulfilling its purpose are also examples of finishing work. Facilitators help groups use their Charter to determine when they have or have not finished their work.

Some groups fail to formally acknowledge the completion of work. They are operating at such a fast pace that they automatically turn their attention to the next task the moment they complete the task at hand. This leads to feelings of confusion, frustration, and exhaustion.

Helping a group achieve closure on their work contributes to its performance and interdependence. Achieving goals that contribute to fulfilling the group's purpose and the organization's mission is what good group performance is all about. Acknowledging the contributions of individuals and members meets an important human need: to feel appreciated. Effective facilitators help groups recognize and celebrate what they have accomplished.

Exercise 6.3.1 Helping a group finish its work

In this exercise we want you to use the series of questions below to help a group finish its work.

Have you accomplished the goal of this work? Is this work finished?

If not, what else needs to be done? Are there tasks remaining that need to be completed? Are there new tasks that you need to add?

If so, what measures or other evidence do you have that the goal is accomplished or the work is done?

What have you learned from doing this work?

How will you formally declare this work done?

How will you recognize your accomplishment and celebrate your success?

Work-out 6.4 - Effective meetings

Preparation

We define meetings very broadly as **two or more people getting together to discuss or do their work**. Defined in this way, it is safe to say that most people spend significant time in meetings. Running effective meetings offers groups and their organizations a major opportunity to improve their productivity.

What is an effective meeting? **It is one in which the purpose is accomplished in the time allotted**. Good facilitators know how to help groups plan and run effective meetings. They create an environment where work can get done.

The average manager spends as much as half of his or her work time in meetings. Organizations that we have surveyed report that as many as half of their meetings are unproductive. This means that managers are wasting up to 25 percent of their time in poorly run meetings, amounting to 10 hours of lost work time every week. If running more effective meetings provides such a great opportunity to improve productivity and morale, why don't more organizations improve their meetings? We have found two major reasons:

- The belief that meetings themselves are a waste of time
- Poor meeting habits on the part of individuals

Some people have experienced so many bad meetings that they have come to believe that nearly *any* meeting is a waste of time. This leads them to use poor meeting habits, eliminating any chance of being productive during their meetings. These poor habits include not preparing adequately, arriving late, not listening to others, not having an agenda, not following the agenda, answering cell phone calls, responding to pagers, and leaving early.

These poor experiences and bad habits can be overcome by consistently using a simple process to plan and run meetings. **We call this process the Purpose-Agenda-Logistics (P-A-L) Meeting Checklist**.

Planning includes getting all the right people to prepare and attend. Clearly communicating the purpose of the meeting ahead of time is essential to helping people prepare. During the meeting, reminding the group of the purpose will help people stay focused. You can help the group set a realistic agenda by asking:

- What agenda items are needed to accomplish the purpose of the meeting?
- Have you given yourself adequate time to accomplish the purpose of the meeting?

Once the purpose and agenda are clear, plan for audiovisual support, appropriate meeting space and setting, food, and other facility needs. The figure below shows a meeting notice that was produced using the P-A-L Meeting Checklist.

R&D Project Funding Meeting	
PURPOSE **Decide which R&D projects will be funded next year.**	**LOGISTICS** **Person calling this meeting:** Vice President, R&D **Meeting Date:** October 25 **Time:** 8:00 AM to 11:30 AM **Location:** Oakwood Conference Center **Meeting materials:** Funding Criteria, Current Projects List **AV Equipment:** Overhead, easels w/ flip-charts, water-based markers **Food/Beverages:** Continental breakfast by cafeteria; coffee and fruit for break **Room layout:** U-Shape for 12 people

AGENDA

Start Time	End Time	Agenda Item	Lead
6:30 AM	8:00 AM	Continental breakfast	
8:00 AM	8:15 AM	Check in / review meeting purpose	Facilitator
8:15 AM	9:00 AM	Review funding criteria	V.P.
9:00 AM	10:00 AM	Review project list	Facilitator
10:00 AM	10:15 AM	Break	
10:15 AM	11:00 AM	Prioritize all projects using criteria	Facilitator
11:00 AM	11:15 AM	Reality check - see if we missed anything	Facilitator
11:15 AM	11:30 AM	Set next steps / close meeting	Facilitator

Participants: See attached list. Be sure to read the information packet mailed out in advance of meeting.

Exercise 6.4.1 Completing a P-A-L Meeting Checklist

Help a group plan for a meeting by completing the checklist below.

Meeting Purpose	
Date: **Time:** **Location:** **Materials to review ahead of time:** **A/V support needed:**	**Attendees:**
Agenda:	

How did the group respond to using this tool to plan its meeting?

_____

_____

_____

Cool-down - My self-assessment and action plan

You have completed four work-outs that will enable you to help groups plan, solve problems, make decisions, finish their work, and run good meetings. Answer the self-assessment questions below. Then, make an action plan to both apply your learning and improve your mastery of the subject matter of this unit.

For each of the work-outs in this unit, rate your understanding of the subject matter:

Work-out topic	Mastered	Understood	Need more work
6.1 Planning projects	A	B	C
6.2 Solving problems and making decisions	A	B	C
6.3 Finishing work	A	B	C
6.4 Planning meetings	A	B	C

What in this unit did you find particularly helpful to improving your ability to effectively use the role of facilitator?

_____

_____

_____

How will you use what you have learned from this unit?

_____

_____

_____

What do you need to learn more about? What steps will you take to do so?

_____

_____

_____

Unit 7
Active Listening: The Most Important Facilitation Skill

Active listening is by far the most important facilitation skill. Only by listening effectively can you determine what task the group wants to complete. Active listening helps you determine how well a group is working together. As you improve your active listening skills, you will improve your ability to support the growth and development of the groups you support.

Active listening is a process by which we make a conscious effort to understand someone else. Effective facilitators are great listeners. As you improve your listening skills, you will be in a better position to help group members more actively listen to one another. By modeling active listening, you will demonstrate its importance. The active listening process consists of three steps:

1. **Sensing** - Using all of your senses to take in information
2. **Interpreting** - Evaluating the meaning of the information
3. **Checking** - Reflecting what you have heard in an effort to gain a mutual understanding of the speaker's intended message

Active listening is truly one of the most mentally and physically demanding aspects of facilitation. In all-day group meetings, effective facilitators exert a tremendous amount of energy using the active listening process. Attempting to understand the group dynamics that are coming into play, while simultaneously keeping the meeting on track, often will leave a facilitator exhausted at the end of the day. If you want to be a great facilitator, you need to develop Olympic-class listening skills.

There are only two work-outs in this unit, but you will need to work on them continuously as long as you facilitate. To help you master the process of active listening, focus on the following:

7.1 Understand the three steps in the active listening process.
7.2 Identify barriers to active listening and determine how to overcome them.

Work-out 7.1 - Understanding the active listening process

Preparation

The frenetic pace of the modern workplace can be a barrier to listening. With people pressured to produce more, they sometimes fail to put forth the time and effort required to listen to others. This failure reduces productivity and weakens interdependence, ultimately leading to poor performance. Active listening is thus more important than ever. Fortunately, active listening is a skill which can be learned and improved.

The first step in the active listening process is **Sensing**. When we listen, we hear the words people speak. We also hear their tone, pitch, and rate of speaking. We also listen with our eyes, taking in the speaker's facial expression, gestures, and posture.

The second step in the active listening process is **Interpreting**. As we take in information, we evaluate and analyze it. We usually do this automatically and unconsciously. Active listeners raise this step in the process to a conscious level. When interpreting information, they strive to understand the meaning the speaker intends. They eliminate the barriers that make it difficult to accurately interpret the speaker.

Checking is the third step in the active listening process. Active listeners check their interpretations of what has been said by making reflective statements and asking questions of the speaker. Reflective statements convey the meaning the listener gave to the message. Such statements usually begin as follows: "What I heard you say was . . ." Reflective statements tell the speaker, "Here is what I think you mean." Active listeners ask questions in order to clarify what they have heard and elicit more information. Good listeners resist the temptation to advise, criticize, or judge when asking these questions. They are genuinely curious to find out what other people mean.

Active listeners repeat the three steps in the process several times in order to understand what someone else is saying. The moment you make a reflective statement or ask a clarifying question, you begin the three-step process again.

Exercise 7.1.1 - Using all of your senses to listen

In this exercise we want you to record all of your sensory information while listening to someone else. Block out all other distractions and make the speaker important. Listen with all of your senses. Use the worksheet below to record all of the sensory information you can possibly gather.

The words; what the speaker said: _____

_____

_____

_____

_____

How it sounded (tone, rate of speech, etc.): _____

_____

_____

_____

_____

The facial expressions, gestures, and posture: _____

_____

_____

_____

_____

What I think the speaker intended: _____

_____

_____

_____

_____

Exercise 7.1.2 - Checking your interpretation

In this exercise we want you to complete at least one cycle in the active listening process by checking with the speaker you listened to in the previous exercise. In checking with the speaker, be sure to make reflective statements and ask questions like those described in the warm-up section of this unit. Check your interpretation with what was intended. Following your conversation, complete the worksheet below.

Reflective statements I made: _____

_____

_____

Questions I asked: _____

_____

_____

What the speaker intended: _____

_____

_____

_____

What message I received: _____

_____

_____

_____

Further clarification that occurred from the active listening process:

_____

_____

_____

Work-out 7.2 - Identifying and overcoming your barriers to active listening

Preparation

Perhaps the biggest barrier to listening is the unconscious nature of the process. We take listening for granted. We take in information with all of our senses constantly and automatically give meaning to what we take in. It is easy to respond without thinking first. The challenge is to listen *actively*.

There are other barriers to listening besides the nature of the process. Some of the common barriers to listening include:

- **Positive and negative triggers:** Certain words, phrases, sounds, gestures, or visual cues that elicit an immediate emotional response from you. A trigger causes you to react before you think. Examples we have been given include phrases such as "team player" and "total quality."
- **Word definition differences:** No two people have exactly the same meaning for a given word or phrase. These differences can lead to minor misinterpretations or major misunderstandings.
- **Personal matters:** Things going on in your life that may interfere with your ability to be fully present and understand what someone else is saying.
- **Poor physical surroundings:** Noisy, uncomfortable, distracting places or situations that make it hard to hear and difficult to focus on the task at hand.
- **Filters:** Your beliefs, assumptions, values, expectations, past experiences, and interests.

Exercise 7.2.1 - Your inventory of positive and negative triggers

Everybody has triggers. And, everybody's triggers are unique. A positive trigger creates good feelings for you. For example, when someone says, "Nice job!" or "Thank you!" it feels pretty good! A negative trigger creates feelings such as anger or apathy. For example, some people have had bad experiences being in teams at work. The word "team" itself is a negative trigger for them.

Triggers short-circuit the listening process. The listener, upon hearing his or her trigger, has a preprogrammed interpretation and response. Triggers cut off the data-gathering activities of the senses and can lead to a highly erroneous evaluation. Triggers interfere with listening because listeners immediately turn their attention to the emotions and physical responses they are experiencing. In this exercise we want you to inventory your triggers.

My positive triggers
Words and phrases: _____

_____

_____

_____

_____

Certain sounds, tone of voice, etc.: _____

_____

_____

_____

_____

Facial expressions, physical appearance, and other visual cues:

_____

_____

_____

_____

My negative triggers
Words and phrases: _____

_____

_____

_____

_____

Certain sounds, tone of voice, etc.: _____

_____

_____

_____

_____

Facial expressions, physical appearance, and other visual cues:

_____

_____

_____

_____

Exercise 7.2.2 - Your responses to your triggers

In this exercise we want you to notice your response to all of the triggers in your inventory. For each of your positive and negative triggers, answer the questions below.

How do you feel when you experience this trigger, both emotionally and physically? _____

_____

_____

_____

What are you thinking about when you experience this trigger?

_____

_____

_____

_____

How does this trigger interfere with your ability to listen?

_____

_____

_____

_____

What will you do to take control over this trigger and prevent it from interfering with your active listening? _____

_____

_____

_____

Cool-down - My self-assessment and action plan

You have completed two work-outs that will help you improve your active listening skills. Answer the self-assessment questions below. Then, make an action plan to both apply your learning and improve your mastery of the subject matter of this unit.

For each of the work-outs in this unit, rate your understanding of the subject matter:

Work-out topic	Mastered	Understood	Need more work
7.1 Active listening process	A	B	C
7.2 Overcoming barriers to listening	A	B	C

What in this unit did you find particularly helpful to improving your ability to effectively use the role of facilitator?

_____

_____

_____

How will you use what you have learned from this unit?

_____

_____

_____

What do you need to learn more about? What steps will you take to do so?

_____

_____

_____

Unit 8
Facilitating Change

Warm-up

Change, whether in people's personal or work lives, is rarely something that causes them to feel indifferent. If the change has any real effect on them, these people will respond emotionally to it. It might be excitement, fear, or even relief, but there will be a reaction. This reaction affects not only how a person feels at the moment but also what information the individual is able to absorb at that time.

Groups are not only at the end of a fire hose of organizational changes, they are creating changes of their own. Facilitators must be prepared to recognize both the changes and their effects on groups they are facilitating. These facilitators must also recognize their own responses to change and how those responses impact their ability to help groups be successful.

Leaders and managers must use the role of facilitator to help groups successfully anticipate, respond to, and create positive change. Facilitators must understand the nature of change processes, how group members may be experiencing particular changes, and how changes affect the work of a group. These learning points will help you develop this understanding:

8.1 Realize how you are already an expert at change.
8.2 Learn how change cascades through organizations.
8.3 Learn how people experience the stages of change: Good-bye, Muddling, and Hello.

Work-out 8.1 - Your experience with and definition of change

Preparation

Change is rarely considered neutral. People almost always have strong feelings about the changes they describe. We have heard these feelings described as apprehensive, happy, confusing, angry, relieved, hopeful, and fearful.

The first challenge in facilitating change is to know what it is. Dictionaries provide a **range of definitions, including (1) to make or cause something to be different in some particular way; (2) to make radically different, to transform**. Everyone makes little adjustments every day that may go unnoticed. Often people notice only the accumulation of these little adjustments. For example, compare family photographs taken some time apart. Notice how different everyone looks. This accumulation of adjustments happens in the workplace, too.

As they recall their experiences of change in their workplaces, most people think of change as radical or transformational. For example, they associate change with reorganizations and layoffs, but do not associate it with minor adjustments in policies. In fact, you already possess a vast experience with change, ranging from those little daily adjustments to revolutionary changes associated with reorganizations or acquisitions. The figure below illustrates this continuum of change. Helping others understand this continuum gives them greater confidence in creating and dealing with change.

Past experiences with change affect how people respond to new changes. There is often a potent history that perhaps includes a major company reorganization, a promotion that created many wonderful opportunities, a layoff that caused hardship to a whole family, a new significant relationship, or the birth of a child. The same change can feel like an opportunity to one person and a disaster to another.

Exercise 8.1.1 - Your past experience with change

In this exercise we want you to get in touch with your past experiences with change.

When you think of a change that affected you, what is the first one that comes to mind? _____

_____

_____

How did that change affect you? _____

_____

_____

Which of the following emotions do you feel when you experience change? (Check all that apply.)

___ Angry	___ Happy	___ Terrified
___ Anxious	___ Indifferent	___ Uncomfortable
___ Excited	___ Relieved	___ Upset
___ Fearful	___ Sad	___ Weary
___ Frustrated	___ Scared	___ _____

In what ways do the memories of the change you mentioned above affect how you feel about more recent changes? _____

_____

_____

In what ways do the memories of the change you mentioned above affect how you facilitate groups? _____

_____

_____

Exercise 8.1.2 - Different types of changes

In this exercise we want you to describe some changes that you are experiencing now. Think of a broad spectrum of changes, ranging from small adjustments to major life events.

What are some examples of personal or work-related changes that you are experiencing right now? _____

_____

_____

Describe two changes in each of the following categories:

1. Daily adjustments to improve your own performance made in the past week:

    _____

    _____

2. Moderate changes that affect a limited number of people in your work group and/or department made in the past month:

    _____

    _____

3. Significant change, made in the past six months, that causes you and many others to make many serious adjustments in order to perform your work:

    _____

    _____

How can your past successes with small, daily adjustments help you deal with more significant changes in your life?

_____

_____

_____

Work-out 8.2 - How change occurs

Preparation

Change is not experienced instantaneously throughout an organization. This fact is often a source of frustration to senior management who have declared the change and desire everyone to quickly adopt the new way. They often become quite upset when the implementation of the change "drags on." The reality is that change is not an event, it is a process.

When this reality is understood, it is easier to see **change proceeding throughout an organization in the form of a cascade.** As each succeeding level receives the news of the change, the people at that level must decide what the people above them really want and what is possible. They implement their interpretation of the change. Each time the change goes to a new level there is another round of interpretation. Those interpretations can extend further and further from the intent of those making the initial change decision. This cascading nature of change is illustrated below.

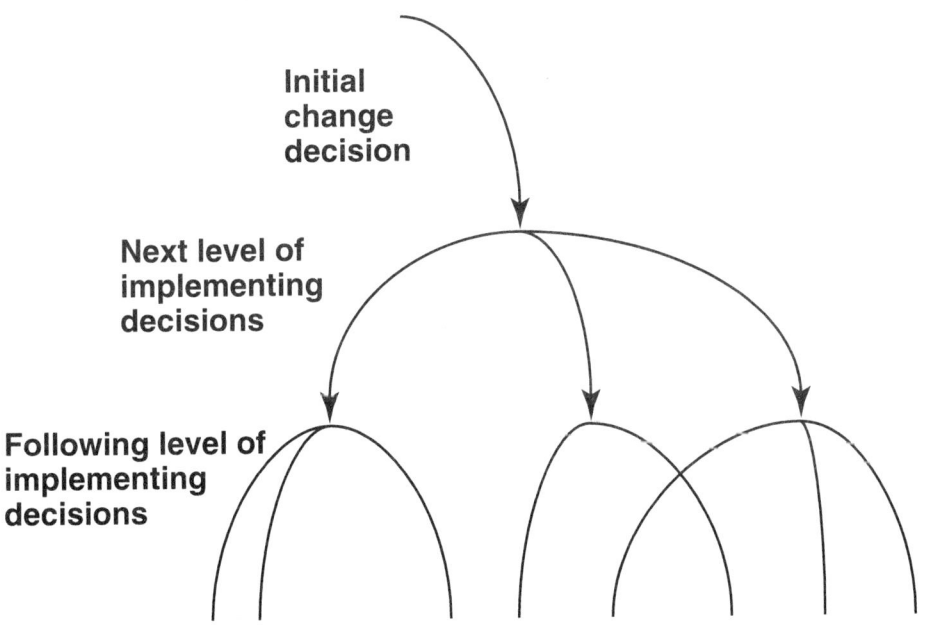

The clearer the communication of the original decision and the more everyone in the organization receives the same message, the narrower the spread of what actually will be done. Since these decisions are often not communicated clearly, the implementation of the decisions can vary considerably from what was originally intended.

Exercise 8.2.1 - A significant change within your organization

Consider a significant change occurring in your organization. Talk to other people in the organization and determine their interpretation of the desired outcome of the change. Evaluate how clearly the change has been communicated. Suggest some actions that will help the organization clarify the change process to produce the desired results.

What is your understanding of this change? _____

_____

_____

What do others believe to be true about this change?

_____

_____

_____

Do you see much variance in what people are doing to implement the change? What does that variance look like? _____

_____

_____

How clearly has the organization communicated about this change?

_____

_____

_____

What actions will help the organization achieve the desired outcome of this change? _____

_____

_____

Exercise 8.2.2 - A significant change within your work group

Consider a significant change occurring in your work group. Talk to other people in the group and determine their interpretation of the desired outcome of the change. Suggest some actions that will help the group better understand what they are trying to accomplish with this particular change.

What is your understanding of this change? _____

_____

_____

What do others believe to be true about this change? _____

_____

_____

Do you see much variance in what people are doing to implement the change? What does that variance look like? _____

_____

_____

What can you do to help your group develop a common understanding of this change? _____

_____

_____

What actions will help the group achieve the desired outcome of this change? _____

_____

_____

How will you use what you have learned in this exercise to improve your facilitation? _____

_____

_____

Work-out 8.3 - The stages of change

Preparation

As has been said before, change is not an instantaneous experience that happens simultaneously throughout an organization. It is not even instantaneous within a single individual. **This change process has been described by various authors as having stages**. There are many models available that divide the process into as few as three stages and as many as nine stages.

We believe that a simple three-stage approach to change captures the most useful information for facilitators. Kurt Lewin, William Bridges, and others have created such descriptions. We have built on their work in developing the following descriptions. **Each stage has its own dynamics, work to be completed, and opportunities for facilitators**. Our three-stage model is described below.

Goodbye   Individuals must recognize that something must be released. There is grief that comes from this loss. Facilitators can help this grieving process take place.

Muddling   Individuals must start at the bottom of the learning curve as they seek to learn the basics of the new way of doing things. This is an unsettling process with much insecurity. Facilitators can help people succeed during this trying period.

Hello   Individuals must master the new way of doing things. This is a time of excitement and achievement. Facilitators can help people celebrate their accomplishments and integrate the new into their day-to-day work.

A detailed description of each stage follows. We need to recognize that people must complete all three stages in order to adopt any change. Facilitators can help people do the work during each stage. This contributes to the productivity of individuals and groups.

Goodbye:

general observations	• Every change must begin with an ending. • It is a time when the success of the past is questioned; why else would there be a change now? • We tend to focus on the past, reviewing what happened and how we felt about it.
emotional experience	• The initial emotional experience may be shock which may temporarily immobilize us. • People look to what was and feel sadness and loss. • They often experience at least some fear: maybe they will not be able to be successful using what is new.
work performance	• Work performance is reduced due to reallocation of energy to deal with loss. • Work performance may also be reduced due to continuing to use the old (e.g., approach, system, etc.) after others have changed.
stage task	• Accept that the change is real. • Release doing/being the old way. • Grieve the loss of what was.
what can be done to help	• Celebrate the old way to acknowledge how well it worked under the old conditions. • Support their grieving while being clear that the old way has ended.
people get stuck	• Unwilling to accept that the change is real. • Continue to remain emotionally committed to the old. • Continue to look to the old to define themselves. • Committed to seeing the old as even more "perfect" than even they had seen it earlier.

Muddling:

general observations
- An awkward time after people let go of what was but have not yet embraced what will be.
- A painful period when people no longer know how to do things as well as they did before.
- Tendency to focus on the present; people are struggling too much to climb the learning curve to think much about the future.

emotional experience
- Hopelessness is common.
- Self-confidence is lowest since people have just jumped from being an expert in the old way to a novice in the new way.
- Individuals are at the bottom of the learning curve and it does not feel very good.

work performance
- Work performance dips to the lowest point due to lack of knowledge and experience with the new.
- Work performance suffers because individuals are working with little or no confidence in their abilities.

stage task
- Learn the basic information needed for the new.
- Create experiences with the new.
- Gain confidence.

what can be done to help
- Understand the uncertainty people are experiencing.
- Provide information about how to be successful using the new way.
- Provide encouragement and confidence that they can be successful again.

people get stuck
- Feel overwhelmed by the enormity of the new and stop trying to learn it.
- Lose all sense of hope they they will ever learn the new way.

Hello:

general observations	• Successes are becoming more common as more is learned and experience gained. • More focus on the future when people believe things will be even better.
emotional experience	• There is hope. • Individuals begin to feel more confident in their ability to succeed. • Enthusiasm for the change is felt for the first time. • At the close of "hello," the emotional "highs" fade as the new becomes routine.
work performance	• People begin to catch on to what to do and how to do it successfully. • Performance finally rises above the level previously achieved under the old way.
stage task	• Perfect doing and being in the new way. • Experience successes with the new way.
what can be done to help	• Continue to provide information about how to be successful. • Encourage enthusiasm. • Recognize successes.
people get stuck	• Become so focused on mastery of the new that they cannot recognize when they have succeeded.

Exercise 8.3.1 - Your experience of the stages of change

At any given moment, we all are experiencing numerous changes in our professional and personal lives. We can expect to be in one stage for one change and in another stage for a different change. In this exercise, we want you to use the three-stage change model to evaluate your experience of changes that are happening for you.

Consider a change you are currently experiencing where you believe you are in the *Goodbye* stage. What are your emotional experiences at this time?

_____

_____

_____

What is happening to your performance at this time? _____

_____

_____

What tasks have you completed for this stage? How well are you completing these tasks? _____

_____

_____

In what ways might you be getting stuck in this stage? _____

_____

_____

_____

What specific work will you do to complete the Goodbye stage?

_____

_____

_____

Consider a change you are currently experiencing where you believe you are in the *Muddling* stage. What are your emotional experiences at this time?

_____

_____

_____

What is happening to your performance at this time? _____

_____

_____

_____

What tasks have you completed for this stage? How well are you completing these tasks? _____

_____

_____

_____

In what ways might you be getting stuck in this stage? _____

_____

_____

_____

What specific work will you do to complete the Muddling stage?

_____

_____

_____

Consider a change you are currently experiencing where you believe you are in the *Hello* stage. What are your emotional experiences at this time?

_____

_____

_____

What is happening to your performance at this time? _____

_____

_____

_____

What tasks have you completed for this stage? How well are you completing these tasks? _____

_____

_____

_____

In what ways might you be getting stuck in this stage? _____

_____

_____

_____

What specific work will you do to complete the Hello stage?

_____

_____

_____

How will you use what you have learned in this exercise to improve your facilitation? _____

_____

_____

Exercise 8.3.2 - Group dynamics and the stages of change

People will enter the process of the three stages at different times. Each person will navigate the stages and view a specific change process from the perspective of the stage they are in at that moment.

In the illustration below, the three people, A, B, and C, are responding to the same change. Person A starts the process in Goodbye and may share that perspective with person B for a time. Once Person A enters Muddling, that shared perspective will end and they will see the change process differently. By the time Person C starts the process in Goodbye, Person A has entered Hello. They do not share much of a common perspective on this particular change. Person A is now focused on the future and the opportunities presented by the change, while Person C is focused on the past, grieving about what is being lost.

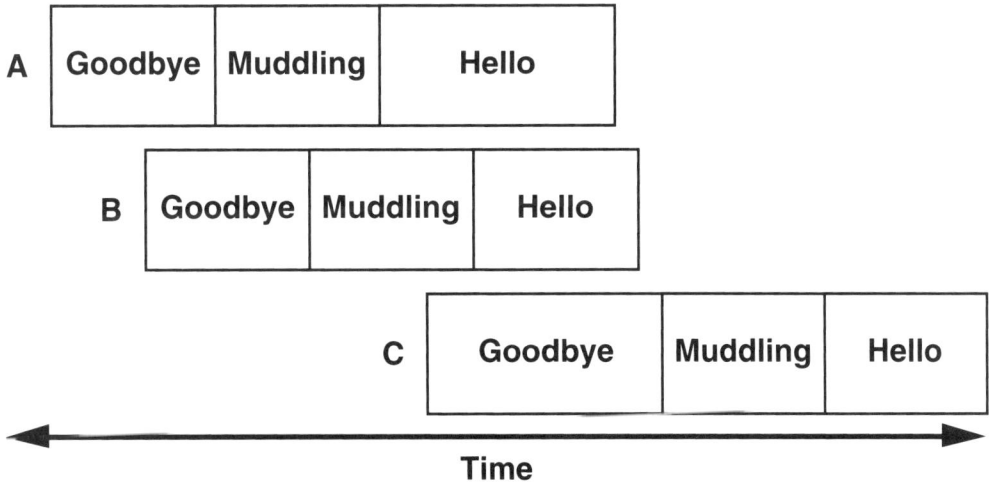

Time

Being in different stages at the same time often leads to conflict, loss of productivity, or even worse circumstances. People interpret the actions of others from the perspective of the stage they are in. In the case of a reorganization, for example, Person A may be accused of "not caring about the people who were laid off" when, in fact, he or she has already completed the grieving process in the Goodbye stage and is simply looking forward to tackling a new challenge. Person C may be labeled as "not a team player" about the same reorganization when this person is simply trying to cope with a loss. Facilitators can help people complete the work of the stage they are in. At the same time, facilitators can help people be more understanding of other people who are simply working through a different stage.

In this exercise, we want you to observe the group dynamics that come from different people being in different stages associated with a particular change. Observe a group for which you are either the facilitator or a member. Identify a change that is affecting the group. In looking for a change, do not forget to consider changes that come from the gain or loss of group members, changes in meeting location, changes in timing of assignment deadlines, and changes in importance of the group's work to the larger organization.

What Goodbye-related behavior do you observe?

_____

_____

_____

What Muddling-related behavior do you observe?

_____

_____

_____

What Hello-related behavior do you observe?

_____

_____

_____

What action could you take to help these group members complete the tasks associated with the stages they are in?

_____

_____

_____

_____

Considering one particular change that has occurred recently, what difficulties have you observed in your group because people are in different stages at the same time?

_____

_____

_____

_____

_____

_____

_____

What practical things can you do to help people in your group understand that they are in different stages with regard to a particular change?

_____

_____

_____

_____

_____

_____

_____

How might you use your understanding of the stages of change to facilitate change processes?

_____

_____

_____

_____

_____

_____

Cool-down - My self-assessment and action plan

You have completed three work-outs that will help you understand how to support change processes with groups. Answer the self-assessment questions below. Then, make an action plan to both apply your learning and improve your mastery of the subject matter of this unit.

For each of the work-outs in this unit, rate your understanding of the subject matter:

Work-out topic	Mastered	Understood	Need more work
8.1 Your existing expertise with change	A	B	C
8.2 How change cascades through organizations	A	B	C
8.3 Stages of change: Goodbye, Muddling, Hello	A	B	C

What in this unit did you find particularly helpful to improving your ability to effectively use the role of facilitator?

_____

_____

_____

How will you use what you have learned from this unit?

_____

_____

_____

What do you need to learn more about? What steps will you take to do so?

_____

_____

_____

Unit 9
Putting It All Together

Warm-up

Having completed the workbook to this point, you are well on your way to mastering the art and science of facilitation. Through reflection, observation, discussion, and practice you have learned to use a number of models to support people to achieve their goals. Your ability to easily and quickly apply these models and theories to your day-to-day work situations will determine just how effective you are at using the role of facilitator to help your organization achieve its goals.

The world's best facilitators employ a variety of approaches to every situation they encounter. It is now time for you to synthesize what you have learned in this workbook and apply your facilitation skills to real situations that come up every day of the work week.

The situations covered in this unit are most frequently described by facilitators we have trained and groups we have facilitated. For each situation, please choose to complete one or more of the following steps:

1. Identify the task-related issues the group is facing.
2. Use the facilitation model elements self, group, and process to evaluate the situation.
3. Identify any change-related issues that are coming into play.
4. Propose some actions that you would take to help the individual or group achieve their goals. Clearly identify the outcomes and responses you *intend* to create through your actions.
5. Describe the possible impact of your actions. Consider outcomes and responses that may be very different from what you intend.

Situation 9.1 - New product line launch in trouble

A team of managers responsible for launching a new product line for a successful consumer products company was struggling. The team had been rigorously debating the viability of the project's financial assumptions. Data from the first test market showed that consumer satisfaction was just under target. Standard procedure was to reduce projected sales accordingly, but the research team members felt they could adjust the formulation, address the concerns raised by the consumer data, maintain the cost profile, and stay on schedule for the national roll-out of the new product line. Heidi Johnson, the Marketing Director leading the team, trusted the research team members to deliver because they had a good track record. Other team members, however, felt that a significant reduction in sales projections was warranted. Team members seemed firmly entrenched in their positions.

Mary Saunders, the Brand Vice President, asked Heidi to join her in a meeting she had called with Galen French, the Vice President of Finance, and Renee Ford, the Finance Manager assigned to the project.

"You know why we are here, so let's get started," Mary began. "Tell us about your concerns with the new product line's financial assumptions."

"Product quality in the first test market came up short. It is standard to match sales projections for a new product line with the overall product quality score. We feel a reduction in sales projections, with a commensurate reduction in advertising and promotion, is the smart way to go," began Renee.

Galen added, "This is a launch of an entire new product line, and we don't want to kill it with overly optimistic financial projections. New product lines that come up short on profit margin don't last long around here."

Heidi felt her face turn red as she heard this argument. She felt betrayed by one of her own team members. Heidi had previously discussed Renee's concerns with her in private. But Heidi had understood that the two of them would continue their debate until they reached a conclusion. She had not been prepared for this discussion, and had to work hard to keep from losing her temper. She took a deep breath, promised herself to look up her recruiter friend later that day, and tried very hard to listen.

Mary replied, "I agree with your concerns about the profitability of this new product line. You know, of course, that we will sink the product line if we do not provide aggressive advertising and promotion support, especially during the first six months of the national roll-out. Reducing the advertising and promotion budgets to the levels you suggest will not provide the support needed to make this fly. We sure don't want to waste money. This is a tough problem! Heidi, what do you think?"

"I think we need to decide whether or not we want to be in this business." Heidi was working hard to keep her voice calm. "Reducing our sales projections to the levels suggested by finance puts us below the threshold that the retail trade will accept. If we can't deliver the sales volume, they will drop us so fast we won't know what hit us. I say we have to keep our projections where they are, and accept a level of risk as we address product quality during the first six months of the national roll-out. We put together an outstanding product development team for this project, and I think we need to give them a chance to succeed!" Heidi emphasized her last point by pounding her fist on the table, a little harder than she intended.

Galen smiled when Heidi's fist hit the table. "Heidi, if we could turn your passion into profit we'd all be pounding the table, with joy! This is a tough one, but I have found some things we agree on. One, we want to hit our sales and profit targets. Two, if it can be done, the research team can make it happen, as far as product quality is concerned. It seems like what we need is a contingency plan as we roll forward. What do you all think of that?"

"I like your idea, Galen," replied Mary. "Heidi, I want you and your team to get to work on a contingency plan. Show us how your team will guarantee product quality improvement and cost containment, and it sounds like Finance will back the current financial assumptions. I want to see your contingency plan within three days. And make sure your whole team co-authors this plan. It sounds like some battle lines could be getting drawn right now. We can't afford that. We all work for the same company. It's OK to debate, but this debate is over. Renee and Galen, I appreciate you coming to us. And I'm looking forward to your continued support of this product line launch."

Situation 9.1 - Analysis

What task-related issues is this team facing?

_____

_____

_____

_____

Considering the concept of "self as instrument," how might the marketing manager use her own experiences to better understand what is happening with the rest of the group? _____

_____

_____

_____

How might differences in style preferences be influencing the group's ability to work together? _____

_____

_____

_____

How is the group's development affecting its work together?

_____

_____

_____

_____

What process-related issues is this team facing?

_____

_____

_____

_____

What change-related issues is this team facing?

_____

_____

_____

_____

_____

_____

Propose some actions that you would take to help the individual and/or group achieve their goals. Clearly identify the outcomes and responses you *intend* to create through your actions. _____

_____

_____

_____

_____

Considering the actions you recommended above, what outcomes and responses *could* occur that are very different from what you intend? How would you respond if your impact is different than your intent?

_____

_____

_____

_____

_____

Situation 9.2 - Nonprofit organization discusses strategic plan

The management team of a large nonprofit with just over 200 employees gathered in the conference room. With little small talk, five executives took chairs around the small conference table. Within a minute, Jim Wagner, the President, hurried into the room and took a seat at the head of the table. "We have a lot of work to do in the next hour, so let's get started," Wagner declared. "As I said in my memo to you, we are getting close to the time when we have to provide the board with our draft of the next version of the strategic plan. We need to take that draft to the various board committees at their meetings next month. I wanted us to get together and decide how we can create the best plan this time. We have talked about working more as a team, so this will be good practice for us. Why don't we just go around the table and you tell me what ideas you have."

Peter Davis, the Comptroller, spoke first. "I thought the last plan, overall, was just too vague. The financial section was okay and we used it in directing my department. We need it to be much more specific in the whole plan. We had problems relating this past year's budget with the elements of the plan. We also have to make sure whatever we propose can be done within the money we will have available."

Don Dalano, Program Director, quickly added, "Maybe the strategic plan is the place to look at expanding the budget. We are going to have to take a look at providing some new services. We are getting a lot of pressure not only to provide more of what we have been doing but to stretch into some new areas. I've got some ideas about what exactly we need to do. Meanwhile, we need more people. We are burning out our staff since we are pushing them to the max month after month."

Ellen Chung, Development Director, gave Don a look of disbelief before she joined the conversation. "And how are you expecting us to pay for that bigger budget and those new staff? Our donor base is being pressed hard by more and more organizations like ours. Our core donors are loyal to us, but we need to find some ways to touch the hearts, minds, and pocketbooks of new groups of people. Don, the services you're talking about won't do that! We're going to have to offer something new and better to our donors. Our message is getting stale. My staff is already generating ideas and preparing to use them."

Sarah Wilson, Marketing Director, looked at Ellen and Don before directing her remarks to Wagner. "Struggling among ourselves won't help us. We have to remember that we have two markets to satisfy, our users and our donors. It is becoming more of a challenge to make the messages to these two groups compatible. My staff and I keep getting caught between the Development and Program departments. I want to see our strategic plan help us integrate this organization more."

Steven Ramirez, Human Resources Director, had been observing with an amazed look on his face. "I may be a new guy on the block, only being here a few months, and I fear I may be stepping on some toes, but I sometimes wonder if we work for the same organization. I thought the current plan was just too segmented. It looks like a part of the plan was developed by each department and then spliced together. Don, I keep hearing that you need more people, but we haven't been able to find time to really discuss what you need. The current plan certainly doesn't help me. I'd like to figure out what types of capabilities you would need for your proposed expansions, but that hasn't been possible so far. I'm struggling even completing my basic workforce plan, and we haven't gotten those issues resolved in previous management meetings."

"That was just the kind of input we needed," said Wagner. "I can see that each of you are taking care of business in your areas. That's good since annual reviews are coming up soon. Steven, you're still learning how we do things around here. I 'm sure you will catch on soon. Now for the plan, I've been thinking about what we need to do next and have laid out the necessary steps for us to complete it. Now, here is the outline we are going to follow. Let's talk about how each of you is going to fill in your part."

The tension that had been evident in the room during the exchange of comments quickly subsided, each director nodded in agreement, and began to read the sheets of paper handed to them by Wagner.

Situation 9.2 - Analysis

What task-related issues is this team facing?

_____

_____

_____

Considering the concept of "self as instrument," how might the people in the group use their own experiences to better understand what is happening with the rest of the group? _____

_____

_____

_____

How might differences in style preferences be influencing the group's ability to work together?

_____

_____

_____

_____

How is the group's development affecting its work together?

_____

_____

_____

_____

What process-related issues is this team facing?

_____

_____

_____

_____

What change-related issues is this team facing?

_____

_____

_____

_____

_____

Propose some actions that you would take to help the individual and/or group achieve their goals. Clearly identify the outcomes and responses you *intend* **to create through your actions.** _____

_____

_____

_____

_____

_____

Considering the actions you recommended above, what outcomes and responses *could* **occur that are very different from what you intend? How would you respond if your impact is different than your intent?**

_____

_____

_____

_____

_____

Situation 9.3 - New manager faces challenges after reorganization

Bob Johnson, the manager of a newly formed customer service department, was feeling overwhelmed. He was in charge of a staff of eighteen people who were responsible for taking orders, shipping, direct-mail campaigns, handling complaints, and managing the company's database. All of these activities previously had been done by three separate departments. Now, he was responsible for making it work, with two-thirds the number of staff people.

Although being given the new job was a promotion for him, he did not really get a chance to celebrate because a large number of his co-workers were terminated at the same time. He said to himself, "I wish I could feel happy about this, but all I can think about is the look on Sarah's face when she said goodbye to me. This just feels awful right now." Staff members who previously reported to the shipping manager, a job that had been eliminated, seemed distant and unfriendly. On the positive side, people who had previously reported to him acted enthusiastic and supportive.

One of his big concerns was his lack of knowledge of things he now was responsible for managing. He had very little experience with shipping and direct-mail operations. He was extremely anxious when talking with the people in these areas. When asked to update their procedures manual so that he could learn about their work, Jennifer Madigan, the shipping supervisor, said, "We are handling a huge work load since the reorganization, and now you want to add even more work by asking us to update our procedures manual? What are you going to do, eliminate more jobs? Be reasonable! Give us a few weeks to settle down first, and then we'll look at this again."

Bob had heard similar comments from his staff two years earlier, when he was promoted to manage the database group. He put up with their objections for almost one year. Finally, he just ordered the group to create the manual. When they were done, the group had reversed their opinion. They came to refer to their procedures manual as the "Database Bible." They used it to train new group members and improve the efficiency of their data entry procedures. Just the other day, his old friend Doug Bowden had told him, "I remember how disgusted I was when you forced us to re-write the manual. I thought it was a waste of time. Now, a week doesn't go by without us pulling it out a few times. And it's a great way to orient new members of the group." Bob planned to enlist Doug's help in convincing the other groups to try it. He just was not sure about the timing.

Bob perceived that the group's biggest problem was low morale. "I can't believe I had to sit through a 'rah-rah' session the day after the big layoff. The CEO was leading the cheers and I just wanted to leave. Looking around the room, it seemed like most people felt the same way," thought Bob. "Well, I'm not going to do that to my staff. I think it's OK to feel bad right now. I need to help them be productive and maybe feel better about our company. I don't want to be disrespectful to management, but I'm not going to stand up in front of the group and smile and cheer. That would feel dishonest."

With his first full department meeting just two days away, Bob was really feeling the pressure. He had decided that he would let his new department settle in for one month, and then have them document their key procedures. Regarding morale, he was open to suggestions. He decided to ask some people for ideas.

Situation 9.3 - Analysis

What task-related issues is this team facing?

_____

_____

_____

_____

Considering the concept of "self as instrument," how might the people in the group use their own experiences to better understand what is happening with the rest of the group? _____

_____

_____

_____

How might differences in style preferences be influencing the group's ability to work together? _____

_____

_____

_____

How is the group's development affecting its work together?

_____

_____

_____

_____

What process-related issues is this team facing?

_____

_____

_____

_____

What change-related issues is this team facing?

_____

_____

_____

_____

_____

_____

Propose some actions that you would take to help the individual and/or group achieve their goals. Clearly identify the outcomes and responses you *intend* to create through your actions. _____

_____

_____

_____

_____

_____

Considering the actions you recommended above, what outcomes and responses *could* occur that are very different from what you intend? How would you respond if your impact is different than your intent?

_____

_____

_____

_____

_____

_____

Situation 9.4 - Production crisis in the plant

"So, how are we going to deal with this mess?" Steve Bishop looked at the rest of the Production Improvement Committee. The Plant Manager, Bob Walters, had just stormed out of the room after shouting at the committee members. Their recommendation for reducing change-over time on production line 2 had wreaked havoc on the process. It had snowballed into a major problem that had stopped the whole production line for over two hours. Walters had been furious. He demanded that they find a way to fix the problem they had created and make up the lost production time.

Now the committee members were trying to regain their composure. The Plant Manager's fury had shocked them. They felt that all of their jobs were now on the line. They had to come up with good answers, fast.

The committee had been set up as a self-directed work team, but nobody was really sure what that meant. Only Steve seemed to have the ability to help the group set clear goals. Even then, they moved rather timidly towards accomplishing them. In fact, this was their first really big initiative. And now they were reeling.

The change-over improvement had worked on a similar line in another plant. They had studied the process for over three months and felt they had a solid solution. They were shocked to be in this position. They all sat there with little to say. In most meetings Larry, Maria, and Steve usually led the discussion, but even they were momentarily stunned into silence. Tom was quiet because he was somewhat shy and much more likely to talk with team members outside of the group. Donna had tried to contribute when she had first joined the team, five months earlier, but had finally stopped when she realized that her ideas were just ignored. The final member, Dan, had quickly stopped participating when his suggestions were met with head shaking and eye rolling. The usually quiet members sat there waiting for the others to do something.

"We obviously were missing some key information," Larry broke the silence. "We told everyone what we were going to do, and we asked for input and critique before we started. Everyone nodded their heads when we explained the process. But I'll bet we weren't fifteen minutes past the line shut-down when Brenda weighed in with her, 'I knew this was going to bomb!' comment. I'd like to shut her down!" Larry was amazed that nobody had spoken up with their concerns prior to the first attempt at the rapid change-over procedure. "We should focus on why we didn't get more input from the line operators."

"That seems to be a good direction to go," added Donna.

"Well, I don't think so," interjected Maria. "I think we need to look back at our own planning process. We missed the key information, so we must not have done our analysis right. Let's look back at what we did, step by step. Do you agree?"

"I do," said Tom.

Steve shook his head in frustration. "We're doing it again. We are rushing off to solve problems and we haven't even agreed which problems we need to solve and which must come first. Things got really screwed up today and we just got chewed out. I have the sense that Bob just stepped on our ant hill and we are now running around in different directions. Hey, I'm still embarrassed that our idea blew up on us. Bob's tirade just rubbed my face in it. I admit it, I'm not at my best right now. I don't think I have really been breathing since Bob first came into this room. Anyone else finding this as upsetting as I have?"

The team looked a bit taken aback by Steve's disclosure, but one by one they nodded agreement. They began to share how the failure of their idea and Bob's speech had affected them. After talking it over some more, the group started to calm down. The sense of fear in the room was transforming into a determination.

"Steve, I think we are ready to come back to your earlier question," said Maria. "What is the problem that we most need to solve? Let's make sure we agree on that and then solve it!"

Situation 9.4 - Analysis

What task-related issues is this team facing?

_____

_____

_____

_____

Considering the concept of "self as instrument," how might the people in the group use their own experiences to better understand what is happening with the rest of the group? _____

_____

_____

_____

How might differences in style preferences be influencing the group's ability to work together? _____

_____

_____

_____

How is the group's development affecting its work together? _____

_____

_____

_____

What process-related issues is this team facing?

_____

_____

_____

What change-related issues is this team facing?

_____

_____

_____

_____

_____

_____

Propose some actions that you would take to help the individual and/or group achieve their goals. Clearly identify the outcomes and responses you *intend* to create through your actions. _____

_____

_____

_____

_____

_____

Considering the actions you recommended above, what outcomes and responses *could* occur that are very different from what you intend? How would you respond if your impact is different than your intent?

_____

_____

_____

_____

_____

_____

Congratulations! You have completed your Facilitation Work-out

You have just completed a comprehensive facilitation training program. You have successfully honed your muscles, putting yourself in great shape to support the groups who depend upon you to help them achieve their goals.

You understand the definition of facilitation: **a process in which a person helps others complete their work and improve the way they work together**. You know when to help people focus on the work and when to draw their attention to their interactions. You also understand the important differences among the roles of leader, manager, and facilitator.

You have a firm grasp of the facilitation model. You know how to use the four elements of **Task**, **Self**, **Group**, and **Process**. You are a master at helping groups keep their task in focus. You use yourself as an instrument to gauge what is happening with the group. You understand the history and dynamics of the groups you support. You are adept at using the right facilitation tool at the right time. And, you are an outstanding listener.

You understand the process of change at the individual, group, and organizational levels. You are a great resource for helping people respond to the changes that are occurring around them. Using the role of facilitator, you know how to help people create the positive changes they want.

If this were the Olympics, you would be a gold medal contender. But of course, working for a living is not the Olympics. In fact, as a facilitator your real goal is to help your groups "be the stars." Using your facilitation expertise, you are now in position to help your groups achieve their goals.

Thank you for working with us through this rigorous program. We hope it has been a valuable experience for you.